Games for Hockey Training

Games for Hockey Training

John Cadman

PELHAM BOOKS

First published in Great Britain by
Pelham Books Ltd
44 Bedford Square
London WC1B 3DU
1981

Cadman, John;
Games for hockey training.
1. Field hockey – Training
I. Title
796.35'5   GV1017.H7

ISBN 0 7207 1246 7

Composition by Cambrian Typesetters
and printed and bound in Great Britain by
Billings & Sons, London, Guildford and Worcester

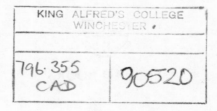

Contents

This book is for Val, Sara, and Trudie

Acknowledgements

Grateful thanks to Jenny Church for
assisting with the typing. Line drawings
are by Tony Young.

Foreword
by Horst Wein

The analytical and reconstructional method of instruction, in which the individual elements of skill and tactics of the game are taught and mastered in isolation seems to have been superceded as the basic starting point for hockey coaching.

In more recent hockey publications the marked tendency of teaching skills in isolation has given way to the concept that all elements of the game should be learnt in game-related activities. This is particularly valid for the following reasons:

1 To transmit the experience of the game which can only be acquired by playing and not by mastering the 'wall pass' or 'scoop pass'.
2 To prepare the most important combination of moves which can then be mastered systematically and applied to the game.
3 To develop psychological skills (e.g. anticipation, the perception, analysis and solution of game situations) which help to improve a player's ability to read a game.
4 To develop co-operation and interdependence between players.

John Cadman, who qualified as an F.I.H. Coach in 1978, has attempted in his latest book to find a more economical instructional approach with the application of the complex method of teaching.

The wholistic approach, in which the match is prepared and mastered by a process of small team games, is nowhere more clearly presented than in John Cadman's *Games for Hockey Training*.

While John Cadman's impressive presentation of the wholistic method enlivened by many small games is a suitable way of mastering hockey by playing, coaches must remember to achieve a balance in their work, presenting a balance of the analytical-reconstructional approach together with the complex approach.

Introduction

Games for Hockey Training is an attempt to put together a number of ideas I have devised for hockey practice, along with ideas that have been picked up from watching and talking to other coaches.

Training activities are used to give players experiences from which they can learn, enabling them to overcome problems they have to solve during a game. Many of the problems a player is faced with require a particular technique or combination of techniques to achieve an effective solution. Through well-designed practices coaches provide players with the experience to enable them to overcome changing situations. The player has to make the decisions on the field; the variety of practice activity the coach has provided will enhance decision-making.

The activities in this book may be used for warm-up, skill training, fitness training, tactical training and competition. Many of them will have a carry-over effect from one area to another. Some of the practices can be used with beginners or accomplished players, some are more suitable for beginners and some for top level players. The most important question a coach has to ask himself when selecting a practice is 'What do I want to achieve?' A well selected practice goes a long way to achieving the required effect. It also helps to isolate a particular area of play. A poorly selected practice can muddle a player, thus diluting the effect.

Coaches will have to apply conditions to some activities in order to achieve the desired result. For example, if players have been running too much with the ball then to bring the point home to them they should be restricted to only two paces with the ball during a certain period of practice.

The activities described vary from practice games for two to those for a group of players working together.

Hockey is a competitive game: players must produce the same attitude during training as they will during a match. Competition can be encouraged by individual players or groups scoring points and winning the practice contest. Where teams are not evenly balanced, or groups or individuals play different roles, the players concerned should take turns in the various positions. Points can be allocated by a target number scored in a

9

given time, or by stopwatch, or by a combination of both methods; as indicated in game 1. Such competition often puts players under the sort of skill and concentration pressure they experience in a game. But the practices can be used, and indeed should be used at times, without competition.

The games have been designed for groups of a specified number of players, and coaches will either decide to have a number of groups doing the same activity or different groups practising different games.

Coaches must allow individual flair to develop where that development improves a player's game. The performance of skill cannot be the same for every player. The most important factor to look for is effectiveness. Aesthetically pleasing skill may not be effective in some cases, an unorthodox method of passing may be better for a particular individual. Of course a skill performed effectively and looking aesthetically pleasing is what we would like to see in all players, but that is a utopia difficult to achieve.

All the games described here have some relevance to team play. Some have more than others, but one thing will come over in most of the activities: wherever possible players must perform a skill and then start the next move, be it to support or to win the ball.

It is hoped that the activities outlined in *Games for Hockey Training* will give coaches a selection of ideas they can draw from to provide variety and thus maintain the interest of the players.

While dealing with the particular points of technique coaches must remember to stress the importance of:

1. *Footwork Before Control*   To have got the body into a good controlling position means players can cope more easily with any pressure put on them. If footwork is done before control, players will find that simple things can be done well instead of making skill difficult through bad footwork.

2. *Vision*   Skill is improved if vision is good, eg. running with the ball well out in front of the body, and being aware all the time of the changing situation within the game — position of opponent and own team players as well as anticipating tactical developments.

To assist readers to follow the drawings, the following key has been employed:

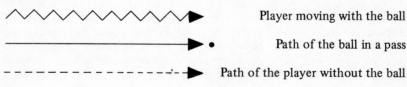

	Player moving with the ball
	Path of the ball in a pass
	Path of the player without the ball

The grid referred to is a series of squares 10 yards or 10 metres square.
e.g. 1 grid
    10 x 10

Series of grids
30 x 20

Grids can either be marked with normal lines or marked out with skittles, cones or other markers. The advantage of grids is that groups can be easily organized and administered by the coach. They give the players a confined area in which to work, making the exercise more effective.

The games have been grouped in broad areas. It must be appreciated that while one game concentrates on a particular purpose the very nature of the game will mean other benefits will also be gained. Continuous relay games in Part 1 are with a few exceptions unopposed games and are designed to improve skill areas under pressure. Young players enjoy the competition against other groups of these activities. Groups can be easily organized using these games. Where odd numbers of players are being catered for teams of three or four can take part in the same activities alongside each other. This group of games is best used with beginners, or as a break in routine with better players.

1   Games for Skill Training

1   Counting Fingers

No. of players: Three or four.
Purpose: To encourage players to look up while running with
                    the ball.
Structure of   Two players stand 15 to 20 yd away from a third
practice: player or another pair of players.
                    A runs with the ball to B. B moves with ball to C. A
                    takes B's place. C receives the ball and moves with it
                    to A. B takes C's place. As each player is moving
                    towards the next, he must call out the number of
                    fingers the player he is approaching is holding up
                    above his head. Players should make two or three
                    calls in each run.
Coaching points: Left and right hand positions on stick.
                    Arms away from the body and ball in front.
                    Body position to enable good vision.
Winner: 1. *Target*. The first group to complete an agreed
                       number of runs, e.g. four each.
                    2. *Stop-watch*. (*a*) The group which completes the
                       most runs in a given time. (*b*) The group which
                       makes 20 runs in the shortest time.

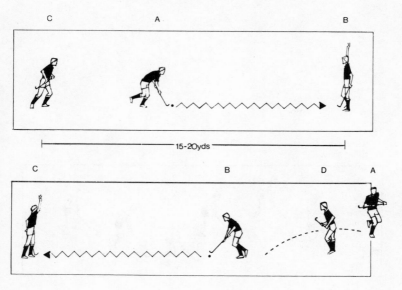

2   Follow My Leader

No. of players:	Up to ten.
Purpose:	To improve vision while controlling the ball.
Structure of practice:	The game takes place in a 25 yd area of the pitch. The players involved move with a ball in line behind a leading player. All the turns and movements of the leading player must be copied by the remaining players.
Coaching points:	Position of the ball in front of the body to enable the player to retain control and at the same time see the movements of the player in front.
	Footwork, body position and the hands on the stick must be given special attention.

3   Last Ball in Box

No. of players:	Up to twelve.
Purpose:	To improve close ball control.
Structure of practice:	Twelve players each with a ball move around in a 10 yd square grid. As the players move around the area they try, while retaining control of their own ball, to knock the balls of the other players out of the playing area. A player whose ball is knocked out of the grid must wait on the side line until only one player remains with a ball in the grid.
Coaching points:	Footwork and body position to ensure good mobility in order to avoid other players and give good vision.
Winner:	The last player remaining in the grid with his ball still under control.

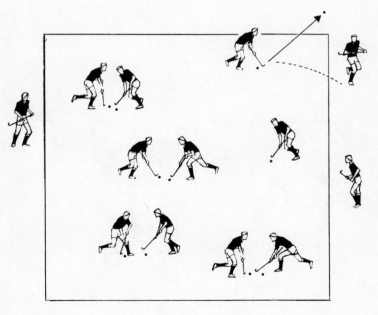

4 Shadow Play

No. of players:	Two.
Purpose:	To improve ball control and reaction to an opponent's movement.
Structure of practice:	Two players face each other in a 10 x 10 yd grid square. One player has possession of the ball; the opponent shadows the player in possession *not* attempting to win the ball. Player A (in possession) attempts to put his opponent off balance and take the ball to either side of the square before player B can get his stick onto the sideline. The player who reaches the sideline first gains a point. Each player has a given number of attempts.
Coaching points:	Ball control, use of left hand, ball positions in relation to the body. Body feints to put opponent off balance. Footwork. Change of pace.
Winner:	1. The first player to score a given number of points. 2. The player who scores most points in a given time.

 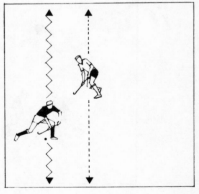

5   One Versus One

No. of players:	Two.
Purpose:	To improve individual ball control.
Structure of practice:	Two players compete against each other in a 10 x 10 yd square using the back line as a goal. Goals are scored by stopping the ball within 1 ft of the opponent's line.
Coaching points:	Footwork and stride length to give mobility. Body position. Creating space to beat opponent.
Winner:	1. The first player to score a given number of goals (say five).
	2. The player who scores the greatest number of goals in a given time (say two minutes).

6   Tag

No. of players	Four to ten.
Purpose:	To improve ball control and vision.
Structure of practice:	The game is played in a confined space with two players linked hand to hand. They attempt to catch those who are controlling the ball. As soon as a player is caught, he stands on the side of the pitch. The game could be played in a shooting circle. The fewer the players taking part, the smaller the area used.
Coaching points:	The main points of individual ball control: hands on stick, footwork and body position. Vision is also important: an awareness of where the 'tag pair' are moving. The players with the ball have to avoid being covered by the pair.
Winner:	1. The last player in the area. 2. The 'tag pair' who catch the most opponents in a given time (say 30 seconds or one minute).

20yds

7   **Avoid the Enemy**

No. of players: Four to ten.

Purpose: To improve ball control and vision.

Structure of practice: Two players move amongst the remainder trying to get as many balls out of the area as possible.

When a player's ball is hit out of the area they collect it and wait on the edge of the area.

Coaching points: As in game 6 except the players have to be aware of the two enemy players.

Winner: As for game 6.

8   Continuous Relay

No. of players :	Three or four.
Purpose:	To improve running with the ball at speed.
Structure of practice:	Two players stand 15 to 20 yd away from a third player or another pair of players. Player A runs with the ball, as fast as possible to player B who takes the ball and runs with it to C. B takes C's place. C runs with the ball to A. C takes A's place, and so on as many times as the coach may require. If four players are involved, two start at each end, the rotation of players being similar.
Coaching points:	Left and right hand position on stick. Arms away from, and in front of, the body to allow a free running position, and to allow the player good vision.
Winner:	1. *Target*. The first group to complete a given number of runs, e.g. four runs each. 2. *Stop-watch*. (*a*) The team which completes the most runs in a given time. (*b*) The team which completes 20 runs in the shortest time.

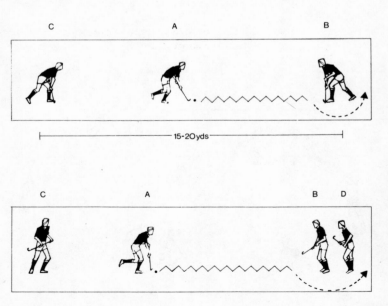

9 Slalom Relay

No. of players: Two.

Purpose: To improve control when moving with the ball at speed.

Structure of practice: Two players stand behind a starting line. The first player moves with the ball through gates, set out like a slalom course, round a marker and back to the start line through the gates. He controls the ball on the start line for the second player to repeat the exercise. The gates are set out over a 25 yd area, each gate being offset from a centre line. The distance between the gates should be varied to make the practice more difficult.

Coaching points: Left and right hand position on the stick. Footwork to get the body into a good position to turn through the gates.

Left hand position on the stick to enable a full turn to the reverse stick position. Ball always in front of the body.

Short fast strides increase mobility.

Winner:
1. *Target.* The first team to complete two, three or four runs by each member of the team.
2. *Stop-watch.* (1) The group which completes the most runs in one or two minutes.
   (2) The group which completes a given number of runs in the shortest time.

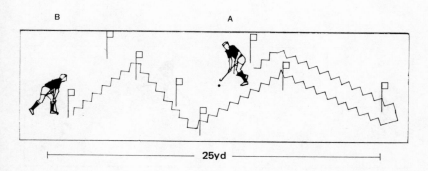

B   A

|—————————— 25yd ——————————|

10   **Slalom Continuous Relay**

No. of players: Three or four.
Purpose: To improve control when running with the ball at speed.
Structure of practice: Two players stand at one end of the slalom while a third player or a pair of players stand at the opposite end of the course. The first player moves through the gates taking the ball to the second player who receives the ball and takes it through the gates to the third player. The first player takes the place of the second. The exercise continues as long as the coach requires.
Coaching points: As for game 9.
Winner: As for game 9.

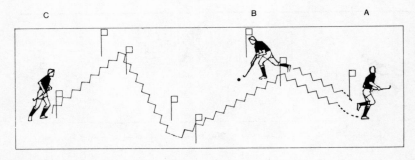

11   Continuous Relay (1) Dribble and Push

No. of players: Three or four.

Purpose: To improve dribbling, pushing and receiving the ball.

Structure of practice: Two players stand 15 to 20 yd from another player or pair or players. Player A dribbles the ball towards player B. Halfway along the run A pushes the ball forwards to B. Player B controls the ball as A continues running to take his place behind B, who dribbles the ball towards player C. Halfway along the run B pushes the ball straight to C, who controls the ball as B continues his run to take his place behind C. The sequence continues as long as the coach requires.

Coaching points: Ball in front of the body to give a good running position and good vision. When pushing the ball adjust the body position to get power and accuracy but not to lose forward momentum. Change of body position when controlling the ball.

Winner: As for game 9.

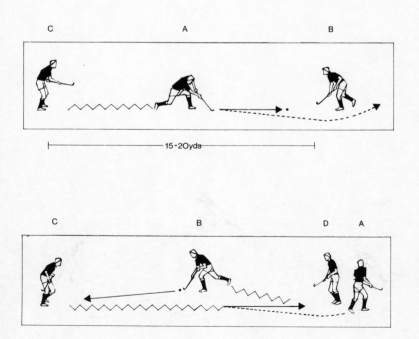

12 **Continuous Relay (2) Dribble and Push to the Right**

No. of players: Three or four.

Purpose: To improve dribbling and pushing to the right.

Structure of practice: Two players stand at one end of an area, e.g. a double grid, while another player or pair of players stand at the other end end of the area.

Player A moves with the ball diagonally to his left towards a point half way between the two groups of players. At this point he moves his feet round the ball to get into a position to pass the ball to the player in the centre of the line at the far end of the area. Player B moves out to his left repeating the movement

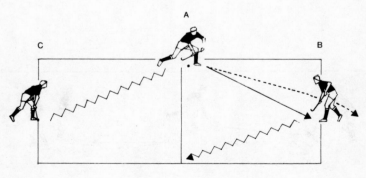

and passing to C. Player A has moved to take B's position. As B passes to C he moves to take C's position, who repeats the sequence. The practice continues as long as the coach requires.

Coaching points: Hands on stick for dribbling and any change necessary to get into pushing position.

Stride length to get good mobility in moving into good pushing position from running. Ball in front of body when running to give good vision. Follow-through to give power and accuracy.

Winner: As for game 9.

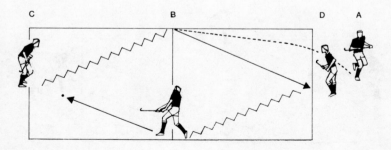

13   Continuous Relay (3) Dribble and Push to Left

No. of players:	Three or four.
Purpose:	To improve dribbling and pushing to the left.
Structure of practice:	As for game 12 except that the player moving away with the ball goes to his right and at the point of passing pushes to his left.
Coaching points:	As for game 12. The footwork involved is not so extensive as the movement is more natural.
Winner:	As for game 9.

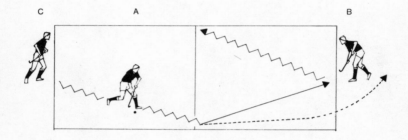

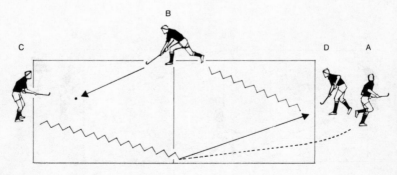

14   Continuous Relay (4) Pushing

No. of players:	Three or four.
Purpose:	To improve pushing and receiving the ball.
Structure of practice:	Two players stand 15 to 20 yd from another player or pair of players. Player A pushes the ball to player B with sequence as in game 11.
Coaching points:	Hand positions on the stick.
	Change of position, from receiving the ball to pushing, led by the feet. Low body position to get a firm accurate push.
Winner:	As for game 9.

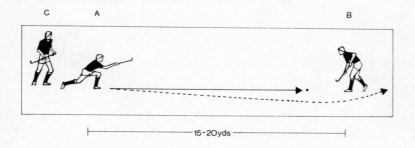

15-20yds

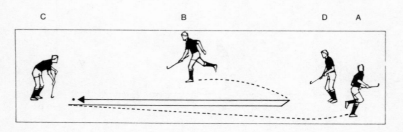

Continuous Relay (5) Receiving the Ball and Passing

No. of players: Three or four.

Purpose: To improve the ability to receive the ball from behind and pass to the right or left.

Structure of practice: Two players stand at the end of one side of a double grid. A third player or another pair of players stand at the far end of the same side of the double grid. Player A runs diagonally across the first grid towards a point halfway between the two. As he starts his run C passes the ball so that A receives it from his left side. A controls the ball, passes it to B and continues to run to the position behind B. Player B controls the ball, leaves it where he has been standing and starts to run diagonally across the square without the ball. A passes the ball to B so that B receives the ball from

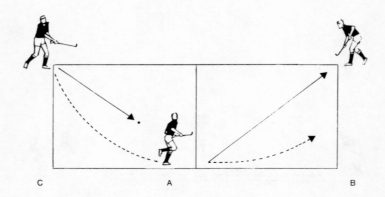

C   A   B

his right side. B controls the ball, moves his feet round the ball, to pass to C. Player B moves in behind C. Player C controls the ball and leaves it for B to pass to him. The sequence continues as long as the coach wishes.

Coaching points: The ball is followed in on to the stick over the right or left shoulder to be received in front of the body. The forward momentum of the player receiving the ball should not be broken.

The timelag between receiving the ball and passing it should be as short as possible. With good control and footwork the movements should mould into one.

Winner: As for game 9.

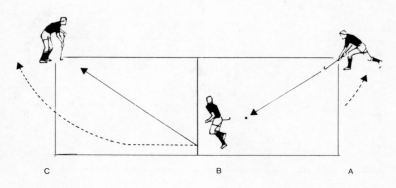

C   B   A

Defend the Goal (1)

No. of players: Two.

Purpose: To improve speed of reaction when losing possession.

Structure of
practice: The players defend goals which are 20 yd apart.
One of the players moves to the halfway point and
pushes the ball at his opponent's goal in an attempt to
score, the defending player tries to control the ball
and stop it entering his goal. As soon as the second
player has controlled the ball he moves to the halfway point and attempts to score through his opponent's goal. As soon as the first player has taken his
shot at the goal he must move back to defend his goal
as quickly as possible, watching the ball and not
turning his back on his opponent. As soon as the

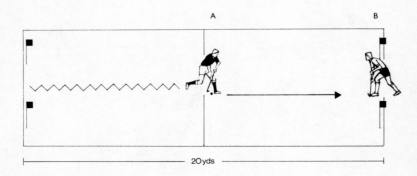

second shot has been made the same procedure is repeated as often as the coach wishes.

Coaching points: To obtain strength in the push shot get into a low position. To obtain a good controlling position good footwork is essential. Change of hand position from controlling to moving forward with the ball and shooting at the goal. Having made the push shot move back quickly to obtain a good defending position.

Winner: 1. The player who scores a given number of goals first.
2. The player who scores the most goals in a given amount of time.

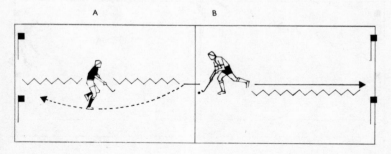

17   Defend the Goal (2)

No. of players: Two.

Purpose: To improve speed of reaction when losing possession, and defend a shot coming from the right.

Structure of practice: The goals and starting positions for players are as for game 16. Player A moves diagonally to the left, to the halfway point, where he shoots from left to right at his opponent's goal. Player B attempts to defend the goal by controlling the ball. As soon as the ball is under control B moves diagonally to his left to the halfway point, and attempts to score through his

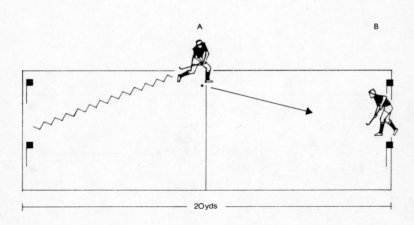

20 yds

opponent's goal. As soon as A has taken his shot at goal he must move back to his defending position to stop B scoring; in returning to his goal he must not lose sight of the ball or turn his back on his opponent.

Coaching points: Footwork to get round the ball to make the push shot at goal from left to right. As soon as the shot is made at goal move off the mark quickly to get back into a good defending position.

Winner: As for game 16.

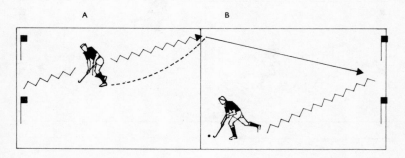

18   Defend the Goal (3)

No. of players: Two.

Purpose: To improve speed of reaction when losing possession, and defending a shot coming from the left.

Structure of practice: As for game 17 except that the player when moving off with the ball moves out to the right.

Coaching points: Position of ball in relation to the feet to get the most effective shot at goal. Move quickly off the mark having made the shot to get back into a good receiving position. Where a player is unable to get back, the ability to use the reverse stick must be stressed.

Winner: As for game 16.

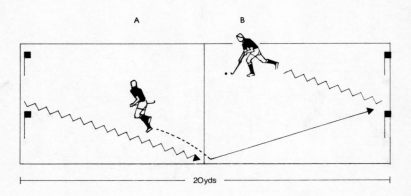

Continuous Relay: Hitting

No. of players:	Three or four.
Purpose:	To improve hitting and receiving the ball.
Structure of practice:	Two players stand 15 to 20 yd from another player or pair of players.
	Player A hits the ball to player B and runs to position himself in B's place. B controls the ball, hits it to C and runs to take C's place. C hits to A and so on as long as the coach wishes the practice to continue.
Coaching points:	Hand positions changing for the hit and controlling the ball. Footwork to get into a good controlling position and then into an effective hitting position. Transfer of weight and follow through to give power and accuracy.
Winner:	As for game 8.

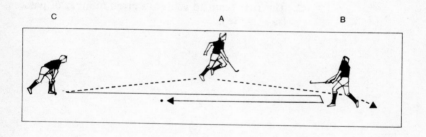

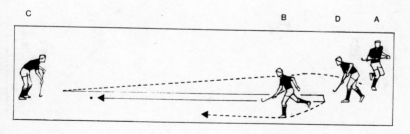

No. of players:	Four.
Purpose:	To improve passing and control.
Structure of practice:	Four players start in a triangle formation as shown below. Player A passes to B and moves to B's place. B passes to C and moves to C's place. C passes to D and takes his place and so on. The distance the players are apart will depend on the method of passing used. Close together for the push and further apart for the hit. The ball can move clockwise or anti-clockwise.
Coaching points:	Techniques involved with the method of passing being used (push, hit, flick). Receiving is relevant to the next move, with stress on the importance of footwork. Stress the time saved by correct body positioning relevant to the next move. Concentrate on technique as fatigue sets in.
Winner:	1. The team which makes the most passes in a given time (say two minutes). 2. The first team to achieve a given number of passes (say twelve).

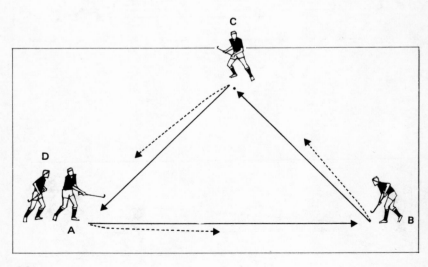

21   Hit *v.* Dribble

No. of players: Twelve.

Purpose: To improve hitting and dribbling.

Structure of practice: The game is played in a grid area of 30 x 20 yd. The teams are divided into two groups of six. One group is evenly divided on opposite sides of the 20 yd area. The other six are on one side of the 20 yd area with six skittles at the halfway mark.

The players opposite each other on the 20 yd area hit the ball back and forth while the six dribble round the skittle and back to the start line. The players dribble round the skittle as often as they can while those hitting play the ball back and forth to each other ten times.

Coaching points: Basic technique for hitting and receiving. Dribbling round skittle and back to line.

Winner: The group which completes the most runs round the skittles in the time taken by their opponents to complete their ten exchanges.

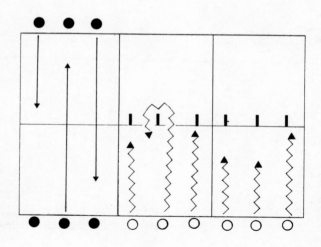

22   Round the Rectangle (1)

No. of players:	Three or four.
Purpose:	To improve pushing or hitting from left to right.
Structure of practice:	An area of two grid squares is used with two flags placed 2 yd inside opposite corners. Two players start in one corner with one on the opposite diagonal corner (see diagram below). Player A dribbles the ball to the flag at his end of the grid; as he passes the flag he passes the ball, using a push or hit down the long side of the grid to B. A then moves along the side of the grid to take B's position. B on controlling the ball dribbles it to the flag at his end of the grid getting his body round the ball to push or hit it to C, following the ball to take C's place. C continues the practice. The sequence continues as long as the coach wishes.
Coaching points:	Dribbling position, ball well in front of body. Footwork to get from dribbling position to hit or push. Change of hand position.
Winner:	The team which completes a given number of circuits in the shortest time.

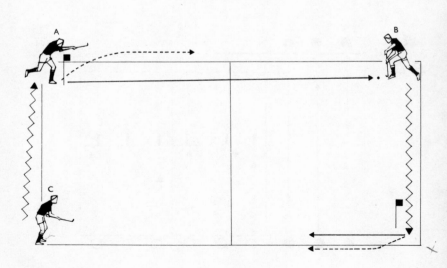

23   **Round the Rectangle (2)**

No. of players:	Three or four.
Purpose:	To improve players' ability to push or hit the ball from right to left.
Structure of practice:	As for game 22 except that everything is reversed to enable the players to hit or push from right to left.
Coaching points:	As for game 22.
Winner:	As for game 22.

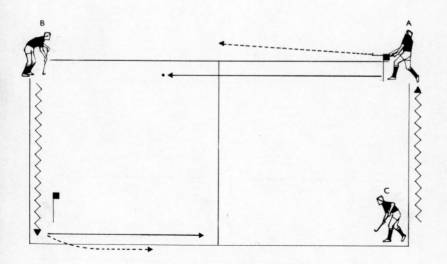

24   Guard the Gate

No. of players: Three.

Purpose: To improve length and accuracy of hitting and
                    controlling a ball coming at speed.

Structure of   A goal is placed midway between two players 20 yd
practice: apart. A third player defends the goal. The two
                    attempt to score as many goals as they can. If the
                    player defending the goal controls the ball before it
                    passes through the goal he gives it to the third player.

Coaching points: Basic technique for hitting. Deception in passing to
                    try to get the goal defender in wrong position. Foot-
                    work of defending player to get behind the ball for
                    the best controlling position.

Winner: The player who concedes fewest goals in a given
                    time.

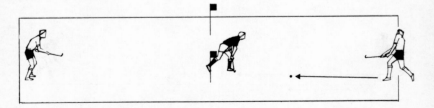

25   Catch-up Ball (1) Square

No. of players:	Four.
Purpose:	To lessen time between receiving ball and hitting or pushing.
Structure of practice:	Four players stand one at each corner of a square 20 × 20 yd. Two balls, one starting with a player at one corner and the other at the opposite diagonal corner. The two balls are hit either in a clockwise or anti-clockwise direction. For pushing, the area would be a square 5 × 5 yd. A player loses a point if he has both hockey balls in his possession.
Coaching points:	Basic hitting and pushing techniques. Controlling the ball with relevance to what has to be done next. Speed of control and hitting to prepare for the next ball coming.
Winner:	The last player to lose three points.

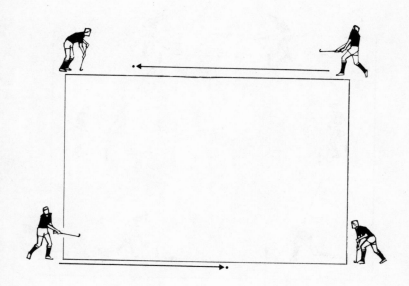

Number of players: Five to twelve.
Purpose: As in game 25.
Structure of   The players stand in a circle marked with stumps or
practice: skittles. If a large number of players is involved more
                     than two balls can be used. The size of the area will
                     be determined by the number of players: the more
                     the players the greater the size. The balls must always
                     travel in the same direction. The direction should be
                     changed. The balls start well spaced around the
                     group.
Coaching points: As for game 25.
Winner: As for game 25.

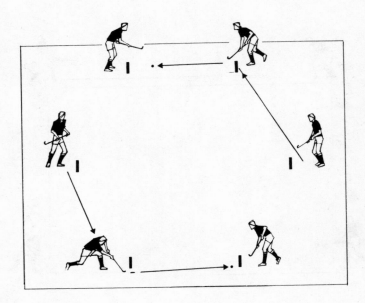

No. of players:	Ten to fourteen.
Purpose:	To improve accuracy of hitting.
Structure of practice:	Two equal teams position themselves on opposite sides of a line of skittles, each line being 10 yd from the skittles. The players hit the ball to each other, attempting to hit the skittle. One or two balls or a ball between two can be used.
Coaching points:	Basic technique for hitting. Speed of footwork from controlling to hitting. Receiving ball ready for next move.
Winner:	1. If in pairs with a ball each: the pair which hits most skittles in a given period.
	2. If one or two balls. The team which hits the greatest number of skittles.

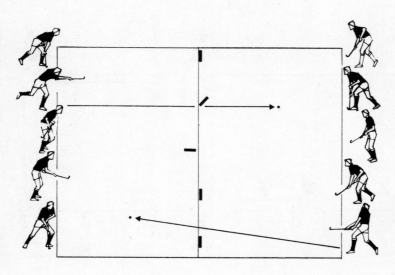

Round the Square

No. of players: Five.

Purpose: To improve control and speed up movements.

Structure of practice: The playing area is divided into half, the whole area being a quarter of a pitch. A rectangle is marked with corner flags in the half of the area between the 25 yd line and the halfway line. Four players play in the area of the square and one starts from the goal line. The single player tries to hit the ball beyond the halfway line and the four attempt to field the ball and play it round the outside of the square before the single player can run to the 25 yd line and back. The single player scores two points if he gets the ball over the halfway line and four each time he gets back to the goal line, before the four players get the ball round each post. The four score one point for each post passed outside the square up to a maximum of four. The single player has three attempts, then players move round.

Coaching points: Technique involving the hit and receiving the ball. Play for the spaces with the initial hit. Speed off the mark having played the ball.

Winner: The player with the best individual score.

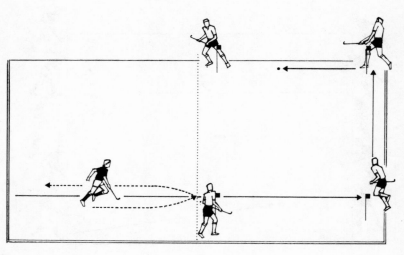

29   Defend the Goal (4)

No. of players:	Two.
Purpose:	To improve hitting and controlling the ball.
Structure of practice:	Two goals are set facing each other 20 yd apart. One player defends each goal. The players attempt to score as many goals in their opponent's goal as possible.
Coaching points:	Change of hand position from controlling to hitting. Footwork to get the body behind the ball to obtain good control, and change of footwork to get into a good hitting position. Ensure that the time between controlling and hitting is kept to a minimum.
Winner:	The player who scores most goals in a given time.

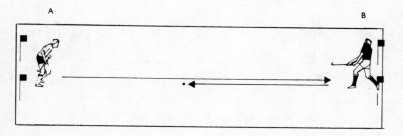

Place Changing

No. of players:	Three or four.
Purpose:	To improve hitting, controlling and thinking.
Structure of practice:	Two goals are placed 20 yd apart. One player defends each goal while his partner covers him 5 yd behind the goal.
	Player A hits the ball in an attempt to score in his opponent's goal. As soon as A has hit the ball at the opponent's goal he and B change places. Player B now defends the goal against X's shot. As soon as X has taken his shot at the opponent's goal he and Y change places. The sequence continues as long as the coach wishes.
	One point for every goal scored. A bonus point is scored if the ball goes past the covering player.
Coaching points:	The change of hand positions for controlling the ball and hitting the ball.
	Footwork to get the body quickly from the controlling position to the hitting position. Reaction to moving positions immediately after hitting the ball. The covering player must move to get in line behind the receiving player to give good cover.
Winner:	1. *Target*. The first team to score a given number of goals.
	2. *Stop-watch*. The team scoring the most goals in a given time.

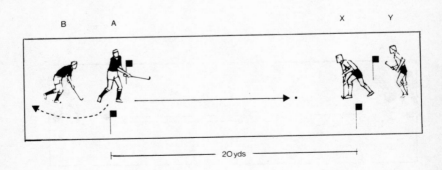

B   A   X   Y

20 yds

31   Place Changing to the Right

No. of players: Four.

Purpose: To improve hitting, controlling and laying the ball off to the right.

Structure of practice: The goals and initial positions of the players are as for game 29.

Player A hits the ball at the opponents' goal in an attempt to score. Player X controls the ball with Y covering him, about 5 yd away. X lays the ball off to his right for Y to come round and hit the ball first time at the opponents' goal. Y now moves to defend the goal as X moves back to the covering position. At the other end A and B have changed positions so that B is now defending the goal and A covering. The sequence continues as long as the coach wishes.

Coaching points: Change of hand positions on the stick from controlling to hitting. Footwork to get body into position to lay the ball off accurately after controlling the hit. The covering player must time his move to get into the hitting position after the ball has been controlled. The pace of the ball layed off must suit the speed of the player moving in to the hit.

Winner: As for game 30.

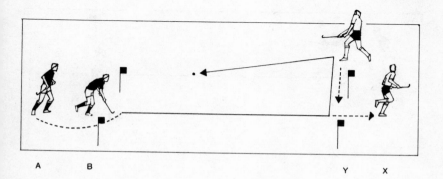

A   B   Y   X

32   Place Changing to the Left

No. of players: Four.
Purpose: To improve hitting, controlling and laying the ball off
                   to the left.
Structure of   The goals and initial positions of the players are as for
practice: game 31.
                   Player A hits the ball at the opposing goal in an
                   attempt to score. Player X controls the ball with
                   player Y covering him, about five yards away. X lays
                   the ball off to his left for Y to come round and hit
                   the ball first time at the opponents' goal. Y now
                   moves to defend the goal as X moves back to the
                   covering position. At the other end A and B have
                   changed positions so that B is defending the goal and
                   A covering. The sequence continues as long as the
                   coach wishes.
Coaching points: As for game 31, except that greater emphasis on
                   footwork to get into the hitting position will have to
                   be made.
Winner: As for game 30.

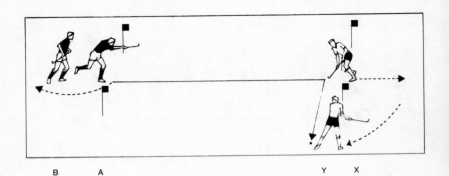

B   A   Y   X

Continuous Relay: Avoid the Challenge

No. of players:	Three or four.
Purpose:	To improve control when being challenged by an opponent.
Structure of practice:	Two players stand 20 yd away from a third player or another pair of players. Player A hits the ball to player B and immediately runs towards B to make a challenge for the ball. B controls the ball and avoids the challenge being made. A takes B's place. B hits the ball to C and moves in, to make a challenge for the ball. C controls the ball and avoids the challenge. B takes C's place while C hits the ball to A. C moves in to challenge. The sequence continues as long as the coach requires.
Coaching points:	Change of hand positions to move from controlling the ball to hitting. Hand position on stick when attempting to avoid the challenge, particularly if working with the stick on the reverse side. Footwork to ensure good mobility when avoiding the challenge. Carry stick in the right hand when running at speed without the ball.
Winner:	As for game 8.

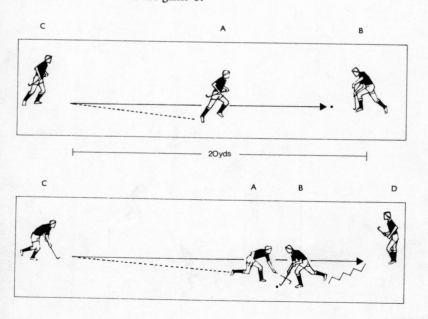

34   Passing to Numbers

No. of players:	Up to four.
Purpose:	To improve passing and vision.
Structure of practice:	The four players move freely about a 10 x 10 yd grid square. Player A passes to B, who passes to C. Player C passes to D, who passes to A and so on. As soon as they have made a pass players move to a new position.
Coaching points:	Awareness of where other players are. Passing to make job of the receiver as easy as possible. Footwork.
Winner:	The team to complete the most passes within a given time, say two minutes.

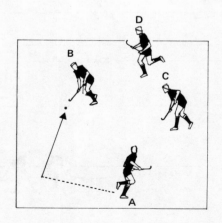

35   Continuous Passes

No. of players:	Four. (3 *v* 1)
Purpose:	To improve passing and space awareness.
Structure of practice:	Four players play within a 10 yd grid square. Three play together against one opponent. The three players pass the ball to each other as many times as they can before the opponent can touch the ball.
Coaching points:	Use of space to make passes possible away from the opponent. Receiving the ball ready to make the next pass quickly. Firm passes give the opponent less chance of getting possession.
Winner:	The defender who can keep consecutive passes down to the minimum in a given time.

No. of players: Four to eight.
Purpose: To improve ball control and tackling.
Structure of   One player is placed in a 5 x 5 yd 'box', the remain-
practice: ing players starting from a line about 15 yd away. The
                  players run at the box at 5 yd intervals. The player in
                  the box has to win the ball from as many of his
                  opponents as possible. The attackers must pass the
                  defender within the 5 yd area. After passing through
                  the box the attackers move round the box back to
                  the start line. Players take turns in the box.
Coaching points: Footwork and tackling technique for the defender.
                  Dribbling technique, the use of space for the attacker.
                  Change of speed.
Winner: The defender who wins the ball from the greatest
                  number of opponents in a given time.

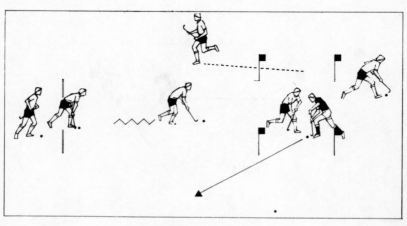

Continuous Sweat Box

No. of players: Twelve to twenty.

Purpose: To improve ball control and tackling.

Structure of practice: Four 'boxes' 5 x 5 yd are placed round a circuit. The remaining players start as in game 36, then continue round the circuit.

Coaching points: As for game 36.

Winner:

1. The defenders who collectively win the ball from the single player most often in a given time.
2. The individual defender who wins the ball most often in a given time.

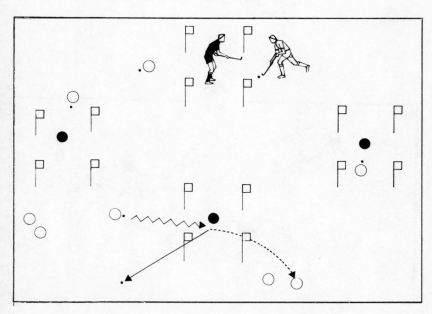

38   Chase the Attacker

No. of players:	Three to nine.
Purpose:	To improve control and shooting under pressure, and a defending role in recovery after a forward has broken away.
Structure of practice:	Pairs of players work from the 25 yd line with a goalkeeper defending the goal. One of the players starts with the ball from the 25 yd line, the defender starts some 2 to 5 yd behind him and attempts to tackle the attacker before he can get into the circle to score. Pairs work alternately from left and right of the goal. After their attempt has finished the pairs move back down the side of the pitch to the start position and repeat the exercise in the reverse roles.
Coaching points:	Dribble position to give maximum running speed. Draw goalkeeper to get a successful shot at goal. Goalkeeper to close down attackers' scoring opportunities. Defenders to get into effective tackling position as soon as possible.
Winner:	1. The player who scores a given number of goals first.
	2. The player who scores the most goals in a given time.

39   Target Man (1)

No. of players:	Four.
Purpose:	To improve receiving technique.
Structure of practice:	One player (the target man) stands on the side of a 10 × 10 yd square, between two markers 2 yd apart. The other three stand on the opposite side of the square as in the drawing, the two outer men with a ball each. The lefthand man of the three pushes the ball toward the target man within the 2 yd marker. The target man receives the ball and passes it to the centre player (the man without the ball) as he pushes the pass, the righthand man plays his ball into the target man who plays it to the lefthand man (the man without the ball). The sequence continues. Each member of the team has a minute as the target man.
Coaching points:	Technique for getting into position to receive ball. Hand on stick: *footwork before control*. Footwork to push ball away.
Winner:	The team which gets the greatest number of passes from the target man within a four-minute period.

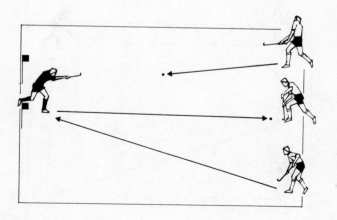

40   Moving Target Man (1)

No. of players:	Four.
Purpose:	To improve receiving technique.
Structure of practice:	As in game 39 except that the target man starts at one end of the line and then receives the ball alternately at each end.
Coaching points:	As in game 39; in addition, the three players have to time the giving of their passes so that ball and target man arrive together.
Winner:	As for game 39.

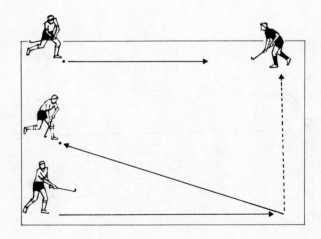

41   **Target Man (2)**

No. of players: Four.

Purpose: To improve passing and space awareness.

Structure of practice: Four players play within a double grid area 20 x 10 yd. Two players start in one half, with the player to whom they are trying to send the ball in the other half. The defender remains on the central line. The two players pass the ball to each other trying to move the defender out of position to enable the attackers to make a pass to the target. When the ball has reached the target the defender returns the ball to the attackers for the game to start again.

Coaching points: The speed with which the ball is moved and the quality of control will enable openings to be made for the pass to the target man.

Winner: 1. The defender wins if he can prevent the attackers reaching the target within a given time.
2. The attackers win if they get the ball to the target a given number of times in a given period.

42   Continuous Target Man

No. of players:	Four.
Purpose:	To improve passing, space awareness and support.
Structure of practice:	As for game 41, except that once the pass to the target has been made the player passing the ball moves to join the target man, making the remaining player of the first pair the new target. The game thereby becomes continuous: each time the pass is made to the target player they are joined by a new partner.
Coaching points:	As for game 41. In addition players must move quickly to support, having made the pass forward.
Winner:	As for game 41.

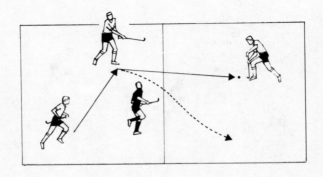

43   **Moving Target Man (2)**

No. of players: Four.
Purpose: To improve receiving technique and vision.
Structure of   Four players work inside an area 20 x 20 yd. As in
practice: game 39 and 40 one player is the target man. The
                    passing pattern adopted is the same as in the previous
                    two games except that everybody is moving within
                    the area all the time, thus requiring players to be
                    aware of the other players' positions.
Coaching points: Receiving ball ready to make the next move: *foot-
                    work before control*. Vision: being aware of positions
                    of all players.
Winner: As for game 39.

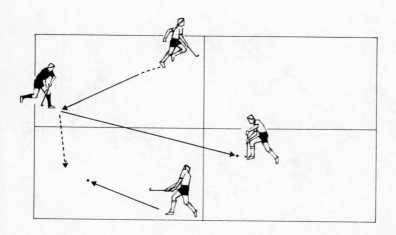

44   Team Target Man

No. of players:	Ten.
Purpose:	To improve team play and penetration passes.
Structure of practice:	Two teams of four compete in an area 30 x 20 yd with a fifth member of the team standing on the end line of the area. The team plays to get the ball to their target man, who may move along the end line to create passing chances.
Coaching points:	Movement off the ball to create space. Reaction to losing possession. Penetration pass to target as soon as opportunity arises.
Winner:	The first team to get ball to target five times wins a game. A set is the best of three games.

45   Aerial Contest

No. of players:	Two.
Purpose:	To improve technique in the aerial flick.
Structure of practice:	Two players stand 20 yd apart, one starting with the ball. He attempts to flick the ball over the head of his opponent. The second player takes the flick from where the ball lands, and attempts to play it back over his opponent's head.
Coaching points:	Basic technique for aerial flick.
Winner:	The first player to land the ball over the opposite touch-line.

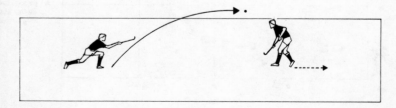

46   Extended Grid (1)

No. of players:	Twelve to twenty.
Purpose:	To improve moving with the ball.
Structure of practice:	Players move around a large grid area of about 40 × 20 yd, working in two groups. Moving at differing speeds and directions as indicated by the coach. The players are evenly divided into two teams starting at opposite points of the area (see diagram).
Coaching points:	Body position for good control and vision. Ball in front of body at all times.
	Close control when necessary, ball moved out in front of body to allow good running action when necessary.
Winner:	The first team to get all members back to the starting position.

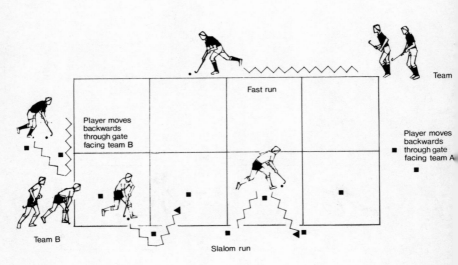

No. of players:	Twelve to twenty-one.
Purpose:	To improve giving and receiving a pass.
Structure of practice:	Two teams compete against each other as for game 46, while a third team acts as neutral players. Players move round with a ball, passing to players and receiving ball back as they move round the area.
Coaching points:	Footwork to get into the correct position to pass. Hand position on stick to get best results. Receiving ball in correct position to ensure forward movement is not interrupted.
Winner:	As for game 46.

48   Extended Grid (3)

No. of players:	Twelve to twenty-one.
Purpose:	To improve skills, beating an opponent and tackling.
Structure of practice:	Two teams compete against each other moving round the area beating as many of their opponents as they can.
Coaching points:	Make the opponent move early enough to create space. Do not get too near before making the initial move. Retain the ball in front of the body to give good vision. Use short fast strides when requiring the greatest control to increase mobility. Use a change of pace in order to beat the opponents. Use as many different methods as possible to get past an opponent.
Winner:	The team in which the greatest number of players can complete the circuit once, twice or three times, without losing possession. (One circuit is back to original starting position.)

49   **Extended Grid (4)**

No. of players: Twelve to twenty-two.
Purpose: To combine a number of skills under pressure.
Structure of   Two groups of players are organized so that one
practice: group is moving round the extended grid with the
                     other providing the pressure and opposition.
Coaching points: As for game 48.
Winner:
1. The player who can get round the circuit in the
   fastest time.
2. The first team to get all its players back to the
   starting point.
3. The team to get back to the starting point with
   the greatest number of players who did not lose
   possession.

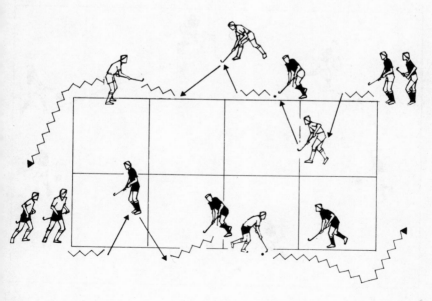

No. of players:	Six to eight.
Purpose:	To improve passing and receiving the ball.
Structure of practice:	Six markers are placed in a hexagonal shape round which the players move in an anti-clockwise direction. The ball is passed from one player to the player in front of him as they move round the area. The ball is received on the open side and passed on to the next player. Players and ball must remain moving all the time. More than one ball may be used.
Coaching points:	Judge pass to help receiver. Receive ball coming diagonally from behind on the left, in front of the right foot. Cushion the ball onto the stick and move immediately into passing stride.
Winner:	1. The group which achieves 30 passes in the shortest time.
	2. The group which makes the greatest number of passes in a given time.

51   Round Robin: Reverse Side

No. of players:	As for game 50.
Purpose:	As for game 50.
Structure of practice:	As for game 50 except that the players move round the markers in a clockwise direction.
Coaching points:	Judge pass to help receiver. Receive the ball coming diagonally from behind on the right with the reverse stick in front of the left foot. Move the ball left to right to get into a good passing position.
Winner:	As for game 50.

52   Flick and Catch

No. of players:	Two, four, six, eight, ten, or twelve.
Purpose:	To improve accuracy in flicking.
Structure of practice:	Two players play as a pair on opposite sides of a net (or rope), in a three-grid area. Each player must remain in the outer third of his area. The first player flicks the ball over the net (or rope) for his opposite number to catch. The ball is then played back to the flicking player. Each player has ten attempts.
Coaching points:	Flicking technique. Hand on stick. Body position.
Winner:	The player or pair of players to get the highest number of catches from the ten attempts.

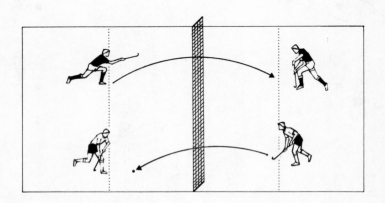

53   **Keep It Up**

No. of players:	Nine, twelve, fifteen or sixteen.
Purpose:	To improve ball control.
Structure of practice:	Players play in groups of three or four and attempt to pass the ball from stick to stick, never letting the ball touch the ground. Players must be a minimum of 3 yd away from each other, so that the ball has to be played in the air from stick to stick.
Coaching points:	Hand position to be most effective. Cushion ball as it is collected. When passing keep ball in contact with stick as long as possible.
Winner:	1. The group keeping the ball off the ground for the longest time.
	2. The first team to achieve a given number of passes.

54   Keep Ball in Court

No. of players:	Eight or ten.
Purpose:	To improve flicking and ball control.
Structure of practice:	The game is played in an area of four or six grid squares. A net (or rope in place of a net) is placed across the centre of the court. Two teams of four or five play either side of the net. Each team has to attempt to get the ball over the net and out of their opponent's end of the court. The ball may not be played above shoulder height. The ball when controlled must be brought on to the ground and then flicked over the net (or rope) by the person controlling the ball. If the ball goes out of the opponent's half or the opponent plays the ball into the net a point is scored. If the attacking team plays the ball into the net its opponent receives a point.
Coaching points:	Flicking technique and disguising the direction of flick.
	Controlling ball in air.
Winner:	The first team to score ten points wins the game. Three games to a set.

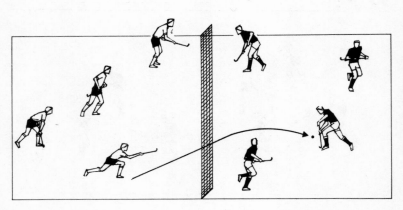

No. of players:	Four.
Purpose:	To improve a number of skills combined together.
Structure of practice:	Four markers are placed inside an area approximately 30 x 25 yd with a 5 x 5 yd box in the centre (as shown in the diagram below). Player B starts with the ball. As player A starts to run to the centre box, B passes the ball into the box. A controls the ball, gets his feet round it and pushes or hits the ball to C. B has moved to take A's original position. Having played the ball to C, A moves to take C's position. C runs with the ball to the vacant corner and hits it down the long side of the area to D. Having hit the ball C moves to take D's position. D plays the ball into the centre box for B. The sequence continues.
Coaching points:	Each technique being used requires attention in its particular area of the exercise. Footwork and hand changes on the stick for each skill must be given particular attention.
Winner:	The team which gets the ball round the area in the shortest time, say five times.

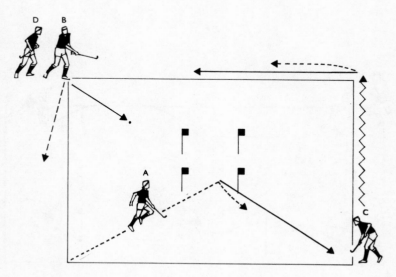

56   **Target Hockey**

No. of players:	Six to ten.
Purpose:	To improve a variety of skills within a circuit.
Structure of practice:	A circuit of targets is set out within an area of the pitch. The players have to perform certain skills at given targets. The area can be enlarged according to the number of players. The players move on to the next point after playing the ball. Having played the ball players move on to the next position to receive the next ball. The game is continuous.
Coaching points:	The basic techniques being used should be carefully observed. The coach should also relate each technique to what has to be done next, particularly to receiving the ball.
Winner:	1. The team achieving the fastest time is the winner.
	2. The team achieving most targets in a given time.

(As well as timing each team bonus points can be won for each target successfully achieved.)

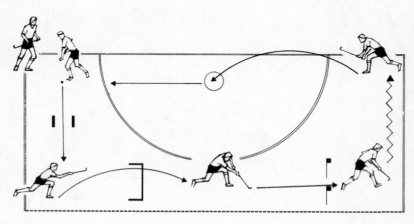

57   Slalom Relay

No. of players:	Two, three or four per slalom.
Purpose:	To improve close control dribbling at speed.
Structure of practice:	Players dribble the ball through gates set out in a slalom course, round a marker and back through the slalom. As the player crosses the line with the ball the next player repeats the exercise until all the players have completed their runs.
Coaching points:	Dribbling position as for basic technique for close control.
	Turning technique: ball in relation to body.
Winner:	1. The first team to finish, if not timed.
	2. The team finishing in the fastest time, over three runs for each player.

No. of players: Six.

Purpose: To improve various aspects of ball control and reaction to changing situations.

Structure of practice: Player A stands in front of flag 1. Player B hits the ball from the start flag (S) and moves off the ball towards flag 2. Player A having controlled the ball lays it off to player B at flag 2 and moves himself to flag 3, where he receives the ball back from B. Player B then moves in to take A's position while A dribbles the ball round flags 3 and 4 and back to flag S — the start. As soon as player B has reached flag 1, player C starts the sequence, and the process continues as long as the coach requires.

Coaching points: Techniques for the differing parts of the exercise. Speed of reaction having controlled the ball and in making move to next part of exercise. Change of hand position.

Winner: The team which completes a given number of circuits in the shorter time.

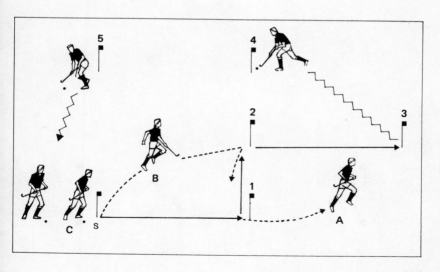

2   Games for goalkeepers

59   Goalkeepers 1 *v.* 1

No. of players: Two.
Purpose: To improve kicking.
Structure of   The goalkeepers defend goals 12 yards apart. They
practice: kick the ball back and forth trying to score through
                       their opponent's goal.
Coaching points: Basic technique.
                       Footwork and positioning to save shot.
Winner: The first player to score five goals.
                       Three games constitute a set.

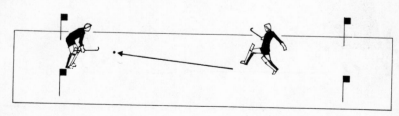

No. of players: Two.
Purpose: To improve kicking and defending.
Structure of   The defending goalkeeper positions himself on the
practice: goal-line; the other goalkeeper places six balls parallel
                    with the goal-line at the penalty spot mark. The goal-
                    keeper at the penalty spot kicks the ball into the goal
                    as often and as quickly as he can. The defending
                    goalkeeper tries to save each shot.
Coaching points: Basic kicking techniques and footwork for speed.
                    Defending footwork, use of stick and left hand.
Winner: The goalkeeper who scores the most goals in each
                    game. Three games constitute a set.

61   Goalkeeper 1 *v.* 1

No. of players:	Two.
Purpose:	To improve stick work and defending.
Structure of practice:	As for game 60 except that the attacking player flicks or pushes the ball.
Coaching points:	Basic technique for push and flick. Defending footwork, use of stick.
Winner:	As for game 60.

62   Goalkeeper's Target Game

No. of players: Two.
Purpose: To improve the accuracy of goalkeepers' kicking.
Structure of practice: Two goalkeepers stand 20 yards apart with a 1 yd wide gate. The ball is kicked through the gate.
Coaching points: Basic technique for kicking with right and left foot.
Winner: The player who places ten kicks through the goal in the shortest time.

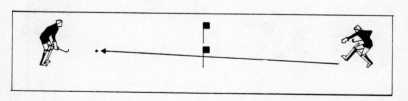

Two Goals in Line

No. of players: Eight to twelve plus two goalkeepers.
Purpose: To improve goalkeepers' movements and reactions.
Structure of   Two goals are placed in line in the centre of a playing
practice: area about 40 x 40 yd. Two equal teams try to score
                         through the two goals. One goalkeeper attempts to
                         defend both goals. Each game should last about three
                         to five minutes and then the goalkeepers change over.
Coaching points: Goalkeepers footwork to remain mobile. Method of
                         saving shots to ensure wherever possible the goal-
                         keeper does not go down on to the ground.
Winner: 1. The goalkeeper who concedes the fewest number
                            of goals in a given time.
                         2. The team which scores the greatest number of
                            goals in a given time.

Three Goals and Two Goalkeepers

No. of players: Six.

Purpose: To improve goalkeepers' reactions and mobility.

Structure of   Four players play against two goalkeepers defending
practice: three goals. The nearest post of one goal being 5
                    yards from the nearest post of the next goal. The
                    game is played within a 25 yd area. The four field
                    players move the ball between each other and attempt
                    to score goal in the vacant goal. The goalkeepers
                    move to defend the two goals under the greatest
                    danger.

Coaching points: Goalkeepers' movement, always watching the ball.
                    Avoid going down if possible. If goalkeeper does go
                    down, ensure weight is correctly distributed to get
                    up again quickly (i.e. on to saving leg).

Winner: The goalkeeper conceding the fewest goals in a given
                    time.

65   **Two Goals and One Goalkeeper**

No. of players: Five.

Purpose: To improve goalkeepers' reactions.

Structure of practice: Two goals are placed about 3 yd from each other in an eighth of a pitch. Four attackers try to score as many goals as they can from either side of the goals. The goalkeeper attempts to defend the goals. A second goalkeeper can be alternated with the first as the latter tires.

Coaching points: Attackers to move the ball quickly and wide to increase the difficulty of the exercise for the goalkeeper. Goalkeeper to ensure that his footwork allows him to retain maximum mobility at all times. Ensure that when saving, the weight is going over the saving leg to ensure quick recovery.

Competition: The goalkeeper who concedes the fewest goals in a given time.

3 Games for Tactical Development

66   Two *v.* One

No. of players:	Three.
Purpose:	To create passing and scoring opportunities.
Structure of practice:	Within a double grid area one player defends a goal against two others: to score one of the attacking team must go through the goal. The single player may not remain on the goal-line. Each time a goal is scored play must restart in the far half of the playing area.
Coaching points:	Move to make a pass possible or to take the opponent away for your partner to make a solo attack.
	Defence position of defender to delay attackers' progress.
Winner:	1. The pair which scores most goals within a given time.
	2. The defender who delays his opponents from scoring for the longest time.

No. of players:	Three.
Purpose:	To improve ability to beat a man and then use available support.
Structure of practice:	One player defends a goal while an attacker starts 10 to 15 yd away with a second attacker 5 yd behind the first attacker. As the first attacker moves towards the goal the defenders must move at least 5 yd out of the goal to meet him. The supporting player remains 5 yd behind the player with the ball. The first player attempts to beat the defenders after which he must pass the ball to the supporting player before a goal can be scored. Having been beaten the defender must recover to defend his goal. The attackers must make at least one pass before they can score.
Coaching points:	Defender's footwork and recovery after having been beaten. Supporters' role to make passes available. Technique to beat opponent.
Winner:	Each time an attacker scores a goal he gains one point. Each time the defender gets the ball out of an area given by the coach (i.e. a grid square, or 10 yd from the goal) he gains two points.

68   Two *v*. One (2)

No. of players:	Three.
Purpose:	To improve the ability to beat a man and then use available support. Reaction of defender after losing possession.
Structure of practice:	As for game 67 except that the defender starts with the ball and hits it to the first attacker, he then moves in to close the attacker down. The practice then follows the procedure as set out in game 67.
Coaching points:	As for game 67.
Winner:	As for game 67.

No. of players:	Four.
Purpose:	To improve passing, support, cover and vision.
Structure of practice:	The game is played over a double grid, with three players attacking one end line A—B and the fourth attacking the opposite end line C—D. All four players may go anywhere within the double grid. To score a goal the three must stop the ball on the line A—B, while the single player may push the ball over the line C—D from anywhere in the double grid.
Coaching points:	Creation of space by the three when attacking, and the reaction of losing possession and covering when the one gets the ball.
Winner:	The side which scores most goals within a given time.

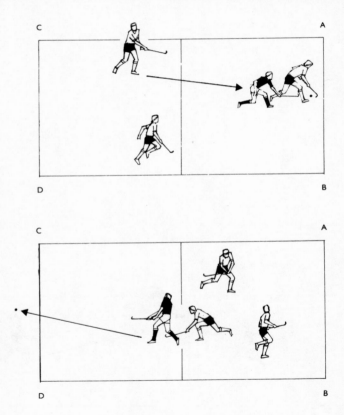

70   **Three Goals: Three *v*. Two or Four *v*. Three**

No. of players: Five or seven.
Purpose: To improve vision and passing.
Structure of   Two uneven teams of 3 *v*. 2 or 4 *v*. 3 play within a
practice: 25 yd area with three goals placed at random.
                    The teams of three (in 3 *v*. 2) and four (in 4 *v*. 3)
                    attempt to score as many goals as they can from
                    either side of any of the goals. The two (or three)
                    defenders defend the goals. The defenders should not
                    be allowed simply to stand in the goals.
Coaching points: Attackers to move the ball quickly from one player
                    to another to attack undefended goal or goals.
                    Spread the game wide to move defenders the greatest
                    distance to get best advantage.
Winner: The team scoring the most goals in a two-minute
                    period.

71   Neutral Player

No. of players:	Five, seven, nine, eleven, thirteen or fifteen.
Purpose:	To improve vision and space awareness.
Structure of practice:	Equal teams play within a fairly confined playing area, with a single neutral player as a member of the team in possession of the ball. As possession changes, he changes the team he is supporting.
Coaching points:	Reaction to the changing situations of attack and defence.
	Using the extra player to create passing opportunities.
Winner:	1. The team which scores the greatest number of successful passes in a given time.
	2. The first team to reach a given number of continuous successful passes (say six).

72   Get Away

No. of players:	Six to twenty-two.
Purpose:	To make players appreciate the use of space away from the ball.
	To increase the use of long passes.
Structure of practice:	Six to twenty-two players on a suitable playing area from eight grid square 40 x 40 yd to a full size pitch. When a player receives the ball all the remaining players move as far away from the ball as they can within the playing area. The player receiving the ball then plays it to one of the other players, calling that player's name to indicate who is to receive the ball.
Coaching points:	Anticipate where the ball is going and move quickly away. Passes must be hit firmly to make the required distance.
Winner:	A player who loses three points first (or a given number of points in five minutes) is disqualified, but continues playing. The last to reach the losing number is the winner.

73   Goldie's Sheep Herding

No. of players: Four.

Purpose: To improve defenders' speed of recovery and attackers' reaction to scoring opportunities.

Structure of practice: Five goals are set, as in the diagram. Two players attack each goal in turn while two players defend the goals. The attackers must score a goal before moving to attack the next goal. If the defenders win the ball they return it to the attackers 15 yd from the goal. Only one defender may be in a goal at any one time. When one pair reaches the fourth goal, the other pair adopt the attacking role.

Coaching points: Scoring opportunities to be created by passing. Speed of reaction by attackers and defenders when a goal is scored to move to the next goal.

Winner: The pair which takes the shortest time to score their fourth goal.

74   Escape Ball

No. of players:	Nine.
Purpose:	To improve vision and passing.
Structure of practice:	Two teams of three play inside a 20 x 20 yd area, with a third team outside the area.
	The two teams attempt to win the ball to get it to the players outside the area. Every time the ball is played to the players outside they return it to the team who played the ball to them. The teams are changed round at the coach's discretion.
Coaching points:	Move ball quickly to give more chance of getting it out of the area. Move off the ball to help your team. Those outside the area move to make themselves available.
Winner:	The team which gets the ball out to the third team the most often in a given period.

No. of players:	Six.
Purpose:	To improve vision, passing and the ability to intercept the ball.
Structure of practice:	Four players play outside an area 10 x 20 yd (two grid square) with two players inside the area. The other four players may only move along the line they start on; they may not move on to one of the other sides. The four play as many passes to each other as they can across the box that the two are protecting. The two attempt to intercept those passes.
Coaching points:	Disguise passes to avoid two players in the box. Receive ball ready for next pass. Pass as soon as possible after receiving.
Winner:	The team which makes the most passes in a given time.

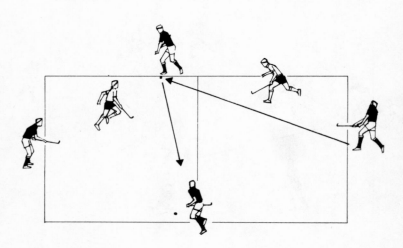

76   Protect the Rectangle

No. of players:	Seven or nine.
Purpose:	As for game 75.
Structure of practice:	The game is played over an area about 30 x 20 yd. Four or five players play outside the rectangle while three or four play inside the area. The procedure is as for game 75.
Coaching points:	As for game 75.
Winner:	As for game 75.

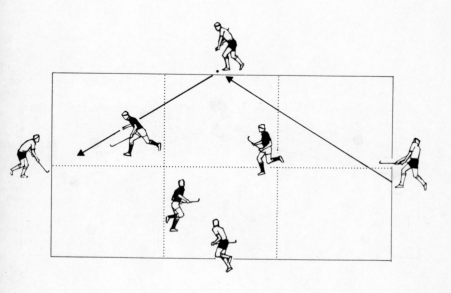

No. of players: Fourteen.
Purpose: To extend range of thought in passing.
Structure of   A playing area 25 x 60 yd is divided into three equal
practice: parts. Three players of each team play in the end
                    sections while two players of one team play in the
                    centre. The ball starts with the black team of eight in
                    one of the end sections. They try to get the ball to the
                    centre attackers who can then pass it to one of their
                    team in either of the other two sections. Players may
                    also pass within their own group. When possession
                    is lost the ball is given back to the attacking team in
                    an end section.
                    Change players round so everybody has a turn in the
                    centre zone.
Coaching points: To increase vision and quick passes when gaps appear.
                    Movement off the ball to create space.
Winners: The two centre players scoring the greatest number of
                    successful passes to their own end players in a given
                    time.

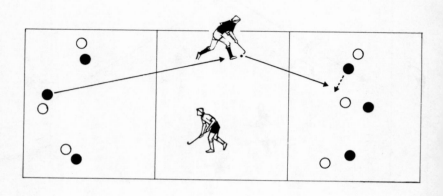

No Man's Land

No. of players:	Twelve.
Purpose:	To look for long and short passes and increase vision.
Structure of practice:	Two teams of six play on a pitch divided into three equal sections. Three from each team play in each of the end sections. The centre of the pitch is left free. Players pass the ball within their own sections until a chance occurs to pass to one of their own team at the opposite end. Each time a team makes a pass to one of their own team across No Man's Land one point is scored.
Coaching points:	Movement off the ball to create space. Possession passes and firmly struck passes to get ball across No Man's Land.
Winner:	The first team to win five points. Three games constitute a set.

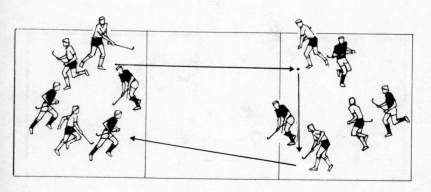

Attack the Goal (1)

No. of players: Five (three *v.* two) or six (four *v.* two).
Purpose: To create goal-scoring chances.
Structure of   Two players defend a goal, which can either be the
practice: normal goal and the circle or a goal put on a side-line.
                      If the goal is on the side-line mark an area or line with
                      markers beyond which the two defences have to clear
                      the ball. The attackers start with the ball outside the
                      circle, or outside the marked area. Their aim is to
                      score a goal in the shortest possible time. The defen-
                      ders score a goal each time they clear the ball out of
                      the circle or the marked area.

Coaching points:	Creation of space.
	Vision-awareness of the position of other attackers before receiving the ball to enable quick release of the ball when necessary.
	Receiving the ball relevant to the next move.
	Shot at goal to be made at first possible occasion, delay allows defence to cover. Defenders to close space down not to commit too early and to give cover where possible.
Winner :	The team scoring most goals in a given time.

Attack the Goal (2)

No. of players:	Nine.
Purpose:	As for game 79.
Structure of practice:	As for game 79 except that a goalkeeper is added to the defending team. The area of play can be extended, as shown in the diagram below.
Coaching points:	As for game 79.
Winner:	As for game 79.

Equal Teams (1)

No. of players:	Six, 3 *v*. 3.
Purpose:	To emphasize basic tactical principles of width, support and movement off the ball.
Structure of practice:	Two teams of three play in an area 30 x 20 yd. No goals are involved. One team starts with the ball and tries to retain possession for as long as possible.
Coaching points:	Movement off the ball to create space for passes or to take an opponent away.
	Use the full width to stretch the opposition again creating space.
Winner:	1. The first team to make six consecutive passes. Three games constitute a set.
	2. The team which retains possession for the longest period of time.

No. of players: Nine. Four *v*. four and a goalkeeper.

Purpose: To create goal scoring chances and to improve basic tactical understanding.

Structure of practice: Two teams of four play within a 25 yd area which includes a goal. Each tries to gain possession and score.

Coaching points: Movement off the ball to create passing opportunities and to move opponents away, thus creating space for others to move into.

Use width to spread opposition. Quick reaction to changing circumstances when possession is lost.

Winner: 1. The team which scores the most goals in a given time.
2. The first team to score five goals wins the game. Three games constitute a set.

Ball Through Gaps: Five *v.* Five

No. of players: Ten. 5 *v.* 5.

Purpose: To improve vision by encouraging players to play the ball through gaps.

Structure of practice: Two teams of five play one on each side of the half-way line and within the 25 yd area. The ball is moved about until a gap appears, then the team in possession tries to play the ball through the gap into the opposing goal. The teams may not cross the halfway line. The size of the goal may be altered to suit the playing ability of the players.

Coaching points: Move the ball wide to create space for the ball to be played through. When a gap appears play the ball quickly through to take advantage of the opportunity created. The team defending must be looking to cover gaps that may appear.

Winner: The first team to score five goals. Three games constitute a set.

Six _v._ Six

Number of players: Twelve.

Purpose: To improve reaction to losing or gaining possession and tactical understanding.

Structure of practice: Two teams of six play across half the pitch. The teams can score in either goal. As soon as a goal is scored the other team take a free hit from the half-way line.

Coaching points: Use of width, movement off the ball. Support to create passing opportunities. Reaction to losing or gaining possession.

Watching for best scoring opportunities at either end of the pitch.

Winner: The first team to score five goals. Three games constitute a set.

Mini Hockey: Seven v. Seven

No. of players: Fourteen.
Purpose: To simplify the game of hockey.
Structure of   Mini hockey rules are obtainable from the Hockey
practice: Association
Coaching points: Basic game related skills. Principles of tactical play.
Winner: The team which scores the most goals in a given time.

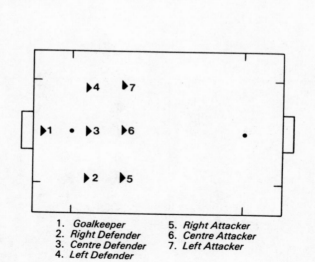

1. Goalkeeper   5. Right Attacker
2. Right Defender   6. Centre Attacker
3. Centre Defender   7. Left Attacker
4. Left Defender

86   Corner Goals

No. of players:	Eight, twelve or sixteen.
Purpose of practice:	To increase space and tactical awareness.
Structure of game:	Players are divided in teams of four, six or eight. The size of the pitch will depend on the numbers playing the game. Four goals are placed diagonally, one at each corner of the pitch. The teams may score in either of the goals at the end they are attacking.
Coaching points:	Changing the point of attack to create space to score in alternate goal.
Winner:	The team which scores the most number of goals in a given time.

No. of players:	Six or eight.
Purpose:	To improve pushing, receiving, and scoring.
Structure of practice:	Two players move about with a bar forming a goal. Two teams (of three or four according to numbers practising) try to score as many goals as possible. The two with the goal try to make scoring as difficult as possible.
Coaching points:	Moving quickly off the ball to create opportunities for the ball to be played through the goal. Technique to improve accuracy of passing. Receiving ball ready to make a shot at the goal.
Winner:	The team which scores the most goals in a given time.

Behind the Goal

No. of players:	Eight, twelve or sixteen.
Purpose:	To improve vision and space awareness.
Structure of practice:	The game is played with teams of four, six or eight on a pitch suitable in size for the number playing. Goals can only be scored from behind the goal, giving players an added aspect to consider.
Coaching points:	Emphasis on creating space.
	Changing point of attack.
	Support and penetration in attack.
	Changing attitude to attack and defence.
Winner:	The team which scores the most goals in a given time.

89   Centre Goal

No. of players: Eight, twelve or sixteen.

Purpose: To improve vision. Space awareness. Support and basic tactical principles.

Structure of practice: As for game 88 except that one goal is placed in the centre of the pitch. Teams may score goals from either side.

Coaching points: As for game 88.

Winner: As for game 88.

No. of players:	Eight, twelve or sixteen.
Purpose:	As for game 88.
Structure of practice:	As for game 88, but a square box goal is placed in the centre of the ground. Goals may be scored from any side of the box. One goal is scored if the ball is played into the box. Two goals are scored if the ball passes through the box and is retained by the team who played the ball.
Coaching points:	As for game 88.
Winner:	The team scoring most goals in a given time.

91   Hit the Skittle (1)

No. of players: Four, six or eight.

Purpose: As for game 88.

Structure of
practice: As for game 88 except that two skittles are placed centrally, in each half of the playing area. Goals are scored by the attacking team hitting their opponent's skittle. Once a skittle is hit the attacking team allows the team whose skittle has been hit to have possession of the ball.

As for game 88.

Winner: The team scoring most goals in a given time.

No. of players:	Eight, twelve or sixteen.
Purpose:	As for game 88.
Structure of practice:	As for game 88 except that two, three, or four skittles are placed evenly over each half of the pitch. A goal is scored each time any one of the skittles is hit.
Coaching points:	As for game 88.
Winner:	As for game 90.

No. of players: Eight or ten.

Purpose: To improve passing and accuracy of pass.

Structure of   Two teams of four or five players oppose each
practice: other in an area 20 x 20 yd. A skittle is placed in the
                    centre of a circle 2 yd in diameter in the centre of the
                    playing area. Each team attempts to hit the skittle,
                    at the same time trying to prevent the other team so
                    doing. No player is allowed inside the centre circle.

Coaching points: Movement off ball to create space. Anticipation to
                    intercept passes or shots.
                    Spreading passes away from centre to draw defence
                    out.

Winner: The team which hits the skittle the greatest number
                    of times in a given period.

No. of players:	Eight or eleven.
Purpose:	To improve passing control and vision.
Structure of practice:	Three (or four) players within a defined area attempt to send the ball past two (or three) other players to three (or four) outside the area.
Coaching points:	Creation of space by movement off the ball by those inside and outside the area. Speed of ball movement to enable escape passes to be made.
Winner:	1. The team which achieves the most passes outside the area wins.
	2. The defenders who prevent those in possession of the ball from passing it outside the area for the longest time.

Escape Ball (2) Even Teams

No. of players: Nine or twelve.

Purpose: To improve passing, control and vision.

Structure of practice: Three equal teams of three or four oppose with two teams within a defined area, and with a third team outside the area. The teams within the area try to win the ball and play it to the team outside the area. The teams are changed round at regular intervals so that each has a turn outside the area. When a team succeeds in getting the ball out of the area, that team changes with the team who passed the ball to them. A new pass out of the area cannot be made until all players of both teams have changed places.

Coaching points: As for game 94.

Winner: The team which makes the greatest number of passes to the team outside the area.

No. of players:	Up to twenty-one.
Purpose:	To improve vision, with emphasis on the use of width, and hitting.
Structure of practice:	Three equal teams play, two teams at either side of the pitch and one in the centre of the field. The two teams on the edges of the pitch try to pass the ball across the field to their opposite team. The team in the middle try to intercept the ball. Teams may pass the ball between their own players to create passing chances across the pitch. Each time a team gets the ball to the opposite side they score a goal. After each period one of the outside teams changes with the team in the middle.
Coaching points:	Pass ball within own team to get opponents out of position. Hitting technique.
Winner:	The team scoring most goals in a given time.

No. of players:	Six.
Purpose:	To improve passing and team play and the reaction of losing or gaining possession.
Structure of practice:	Three teams of two each play within a double grid area (about 10 x 20 yd). Two teams, A and B start on the playing area. Team A has possession of the ball and team C starts behind A's goal-line. One of team B must be in the goal until his team win possession, or a goal is scored against them. As soon as B gets possession or A scores a goal, B becomes the attacking team. Immediately this happens A goes behind B's goal-line and C comes on to the pitch as the defending team, one of them going into goal until they gain possession. When C gains possession A moves on to become the defending team, and B moves behind the line they were attacking, and so on.
Coaching points:	Speed of reaction to the changing situation. Aspects of passing and creating space. Defenders closing players down.
Winner:	The team scoring most goals within a given time, say five or ten minutes.

Team B   Team A   Team C

No. of players:	Nine.
Purpose:	As for game 97.
Structure of practice:	As for game 97, except that there are three players in each team. As each team moves on to the pitch it will have one player in goal and two outside. The playing area is enlarged to approximately six grid squares, i.e. 20 x 30 yd.
Coaching points:	As for game 97.
Winner:	As for game 97.

Team B   Team A   Team C

Three-Team Games (3)

Number of players: Twelve or fifteen.

Purpose: As for game 97.

Structure of practice: As for game 97, except that each team as it moves on to the pitch will have three (or four) players outside the goal. The playing area now becomes the area from the halfway line to the 25 yd line.

Coaching points: As for game 97.

Winner: As for game 97.

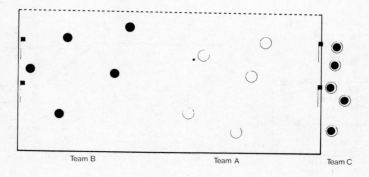

Team B   Team A   Team C

100   **Three-Team Games (4)**

No. of players: Eighteen or twenty-one.
Purpose: As for game 97.
Structure of As for game 97, except that each team will have five
practice: (or six) players on the field with one in the goal.
When a team loses possession in the opponent's
defending area they attempt to regain the ball and
continue their attack. However as soon as the ball is
moved into the other half of the pitch the team
tackling back must retire behind the line they were
attacking and the team off the field moves on as the
new defending team.
Coaching points: As for game 97 plus the reaction to losing possession
by tackling back. Because tackling back becomes part
of the game, fast counterattack is important to offset
the effect of players tackling back.
Winner: As for game 97.

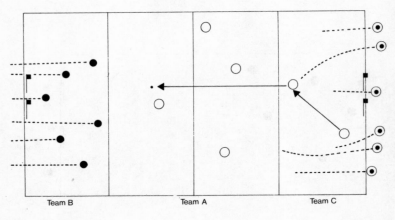

Conditioned Games (1) Two or Three-Touch Hockey

No. of players:	Five to twenty-two.
Purpose:	To improve vision, control and passing.
Structure of practice:	Teams (equal or unequal) play on a pitch of suitable size; if three against two, two grid squares is sufficient; if eleven a side, then a full sized pitch. Each player is only allowed two or three touches of the ball in controlling and passing to the next player. Two touches is more difficult than three, the latter being more suitable for the less good player. A free hit is given to the opponents when a player plays the ball more than the allowed times.
Coaching points:	Players must use their vision to enable them to get into a receiving position that will make their pass to the next player easier to perform.
	The *first touch on the ball is the critical one*: full control must be made immediately.
Winner:	1. The team which makes most consecutive passes.
	2. The team which scores the greatest number of goals in a given time.

No. of players:	Five to twenty-two.
Purpose:	To encourage players to react in attack when a pass has been made. To share responsibility for a player who has moved out of position.
Structure of practice:	Teams play as for a normal small team or full team game. Each time a player makes a pass to one of his own team he must overlap that player to be available for another pass. The player receiving the ball may use the overlapping player or may pass to any member of his team.
Coaching points:	As soon as a pass is made, react immediately to take up a new attacking position. Movement off the ball involves two things. (1) It creates space for the moving player or for another player. (2) When a player has overlapped, other players must cover the player who has gone into attack.
Winner:	As for game 101.

103   **Conditioned Games (3) Passing — Two Forward One Back**

No. of players: Six to twenty-two.
Purpose: To make players aware that good possession may
                  mean varying the direction of passing.
Structure of   Two teams of equal numbers play either a small team
practice: or full team game. After every second pass made
                  forwards one must be played back.
Coaching points: Awareness of changing the direction of play and
                  anticipating to cope with that change. Players moving
                  off-the-ball to make passes possible, and to create
                  space for passes.
Winner: As for game 101.

104   **Conditioned Games (4) Passing — Square and Through**

No. of players: As for game 103.
Purpose: As for game 103 with the addition of making players
                     aware of playing the ball forwards into space.
Structure of   As for game 103 except that every square pass has to
practice: be followed by a through pass.
Coaching points: As for game 103.
Winner: As for game 101.

No. of players:	Six to twelve.
Purpose:	To retain possession of the ball for as long as possible.
Structure of practice:	Teams may be equal or unequal, according to the particular emphasis the coach wishes to place. No goals are used — players attempt to retain possession of the ball as long as possible and to make as many passes as possible in retaining possession.
Coaching points:	Movement off the ball to create passing opportunities. Diagonal running and a preparedness to move out of position to make passes possible. Long passes may be required to put the ball into safer areas of the pitch where good possession can be maintained. Passes in all directions must be employed.
Winner:	1. The team which makes most consecutive passes.
	2. The team which keeps possession for the longest time.

No. of players:	Nine to twelve.
Purpose:	To improve effectiveness of penetration.
Structure of practice:	Two teams play in one half of a given area, while a goalkeeper defends a goal in the other half. Each team attempts to get the ball over the halfway area to one of its forwards, who moves onto the ball and attempts to score in the goal. Only the teams whose players are in possession may cross the halfway line before the ball. The opponents may only cross the line after the ball has crossed to attempt to stop the attackers scoring.
Coaching points:	Creation of space to make passes possible. Anticipation of pass and moving forward into space.
Winner:	The team which scores the greatest number of goals in a given time period.

107   **Around Posts**

No. of players:	Eight.
Purpose:	To improve the appreciation of using width.
Structure of practice:	Four players play in one half of an area 20 × 20 yd with one opponent, while two players play in the other half with one opponent. The four pass the ball between each other, attempting to make a pass to one of the two. A player who receives the ball must move outside one of the posts and dribble it over the back line or pass it to his team mate to dribble it over. The one opponent in the first half attempts to stop the players making passes to their colleagues, while the one attempts to stop one of the two dribbling over the line. Change players round to ensure that each has a turn in the various parts of the game.
Coaching points:	The creation of space. Receiving ball relevant to next move. Basic technique points in method of pass adopted. Use of width to spread opponents out make them less effective.
Winner:	The player who dribbles the ball most often over the back line is the winner.

108   Seven *v.* Seven: Wingers Game

No. of players: Fourteen.

Purpose: To increase players' ability to spread their attacks wide.

Structure of practice: Two teams of seven aside play on a full size pitch. In addition to the goals at either end of the field four goals are placed 10 yd wide, 16 yd out from each goal line with one post on the side line. Before any team can score, their attack must have passed through one of the wing goals, either by a pass or a player dribbling through the goal, in the half that the team is attacking. No goal can be scored until the attack has passed through a wing goal.

Coaching points: Use the cross pass to create space to penetrate through the wing goal. Movement off the ball to create space. Quick reaction of all players to losing possession and defending as a team.

Winner: The team which scores most goals in a given time.

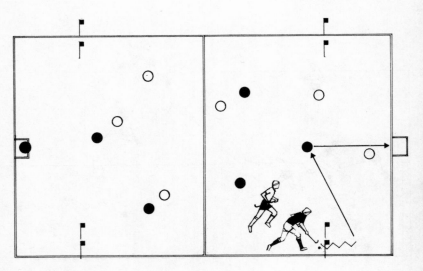

109   Interchange Places (1)

No. of players: Ten.

Purpose: To help players to understand that when a player moves out of position another player has got to be prepared to fill the gap or cover.

Structure of practice: Two teams of five play across a pitch within the 25 yd area.

Coaching points: Players must be aware of the movement of their own players as well as of the ball. Vision. Other players should move the ball into the spaces created for their team members.

Winner: The team which scores the most goals in a given time.

110   Interchange Places (2)

No. of players:	Fourteen, sixteen, eighteen or twenty.
Purpose:	As for game 109.
Structure of practice:	Two teams of seven (eight, nine or ten) play on a full pitch.
Coaching points:	As for game 109.
Winner:	As for game 109.

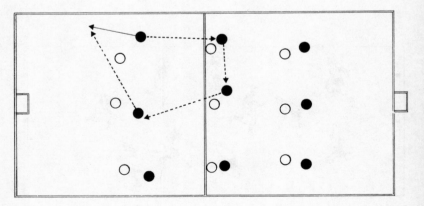

111   Vacant Grids

No. of players:	Eight, ten or twelve.
Purpose:	To move out of own area into space to create passing opportunities.
Structure of practice:	Four, five or six aside in a grid area that leaves two or three vacant squares. No more than one player from each team can be in one square at any one time.
Coaching points:	Players to be made aware that by moving to a new position they can make themselves available for a pass which will be played into a vacant space.
Winner:	1. The side which makes most consecutive passes in a given time. 2. The first team to achieve five consecutive passes.

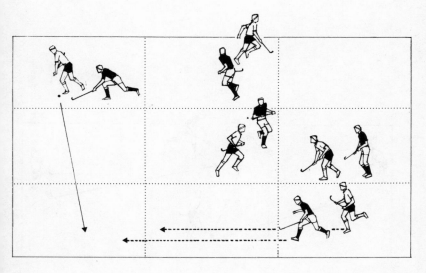

Continuous Passing and Free Hits

No. of players:	Five.
Purpose:	To improve ability to retain possession from free hits.
Structure of practice:	An area of three grid squares is used, with two players on the outer side of the end grids. The attackers and a defender play in the middle third. One of the players, A, in the outer squares starts with the ball as though taking a free hit; he must hit the ball to one of the attackers in the middle third. The two attackers in the middle third must then make at least one pass before playing the ball to the other player, B, in the outer third. The defender tries to intercept the ball or tackle the players in the middle third. The game is then repeated with B taking the free hit.
Coaching points:	A and B should disguise their hit to make it more difficult for the defender. The attackers must control the ball in relation to what they have to do next.
Winner:	The group which gets the ball from A to B and back most often in a given period.

113   Delay the Attack (1)

No. of players: Three.

Purpose: To improve defender's ability to close down attackers
                   and delay opponents' progress.

Structure of   Two players start at the end of a double grid while a
practice: defender stands on the half way line. The two players
                   attempt to get the ball to the far end of the double
                   grid, while the defender attempts to delay them as
                   long as possible, or win the ball.

Coaching points: Footwork to enable defender:—
                   (a) To change position quickly.
                   (b) To recover if beaten.
                   (c) To move into a strong tackle.
                   Attackers to move the ball quickly using the full
                   width of the grid to make the defender's job more
                   difficult.

Winner: The defender who delays the attackers for the longest
                   time.

114   Delay the Attack (2)

No. of players:	Five.
Purpose:	To improve defenders' ability to work together to delay an attack and delay opponents' progress.
Structure of practice:	Three players start with the ball in a grid area, (or area 30 × 20 yd). The two defenders start in the middle third of the area. They have to delay the attackers getting the ball to the far end of the area, or win the ball from them.
Coaching points:	To ensure the best results the defender on whose side the ball is closes the attacker down, while the other defender covers, but is in a position to move in towards the ball if it is passed across the area. Defenders must share the responsibility. Attackers to use the width of the area to make defenders' job more difficult.
Winner:	As for game 113.

115   Delay the Attack (3)

No. of players: Seven, or any uneven number up to twenty-one.
Purpose: As for game 114.
Structure of
practice: As for game 114 except the game is played across
the pitch in one of the 25 yd areas.
Coaching points: As for game 114.
Winner: As for game 113.

No. of players:	Six.
Purpose:	To instill defensive discipline, organization and an awareness of player's responsibilities within a defence.
Structure of practice:	Two teams of three play in a fairly restricted area, e.g. 15 x 25 yd, each team defending a goal. The team losing possession must immediately form a triangular pattern on their own goal side of the ball. Their position will vary according to the play of the attacking team.
Coaching points:	Form triangle pattern as quickly as possible. The player nearest to the ball closes the attacker down. The back man of the triangle gives cover to the front two, while the third man gives cover across the playing area.
Winner:	The side conceding the fewest goals in a given time.

117   Pattern Play (2) Diamond

No. of players:	Eight.
Purpose:	As in game 116.
Structure of practice:	Two teams of four play in a restricted area, e.g. six-grid square 20 x 30 yd, or an area 20 yd wide and 25 yd long; this fits in with the markings on the pitch and groups can be arranged so that they do not clash. As for game 116. As soon as possession is lost a diamond pattern is formed on the goal side of the ball.
Coaching points:	Form diamonds as fast as possible. There are now two triangles, and players must learn their roles for both marking and covering. Those players nearest to the ball must move in to close down their opponents, while those away from the ball give cover.
Winner:	As for game 116.

No. of players:	Ten.
Purpose:	As for game 116 emphasizing the increasing responsibility to other players as the numbers in the team increase.
Structure of practice:	Two teams of five playing over the pitch in the 25 yd to halfway area. As for game 116, but as soon as possession is lost a star pattern is formed immediately on the goal side of the ball.
Coaching points:	As for game 116, emphasizing the triangles and players' covering and marking responsibility.
Winner:	As for game 116.

Pattern Play (4) Pyramid

No. of players:	Twelve.
Purpose:	As for game 116.
Structure of practice:	Two teams of six playing across the pitch in the area between the 25 yd and halfway lines. As soon as possession is lost the players form a pyramid on their goal side of the ball.
Coaching points:	As for game 116.
Winner:	As for game 116.

No. of players:	Fourteen.
Purpose:	As for game 119, with the addition of attacker's role in defence added to the pattern being used. (The additional player on each side could be used with the earlier patterns; however, in the early stage make the practice as simple to follow as possible.)
Structure of practice:	Two teams of seven playing across the pitch in the area between the 25 yd and halfway lines. As soon as possession is lost six of the players form a pyramid pattern while the seventh harries and hurries the opposition into making a mistake.
Coaching points:	As in game 116, plus the role in defence of the forward player. His reaction will, if successful, relieve the pressure on the defending player.
Winner:	As for game 116.

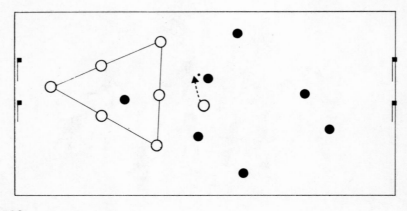

No. of players:	Sixteen.
Purpose:	As in game 120 except that here there are two attackers.
Structure of practice:	Two teams of eight playing on the full length of the pitch. When possession is lost six players form a pyramid, while two forward players do the harrying and chasing.
Coaching points:	As for game 120, plus the role of the two forward players. The nearest to the ball does the harrying and chasing while the other covers possible moves across the pitch the opposition might make.
Winner:	As for game 116.

122   Pattern Play (7) Pyramid plus Three and Four

No. of players:	Eighteen or twenty.
Purpose:	As in game 120 except that there are now three attackers (eighteen players) and (with twenty players) a further defender. The next stage is to add a goal-keeper and go into full game.
Coaching points:	As in game 120, plus the role of the three attacking men in defence. Harrying and chasing must be stressed and the need to take responsibility for a defender. Anticipation of opponents cross-field passes.
Winner:	As in game 116.

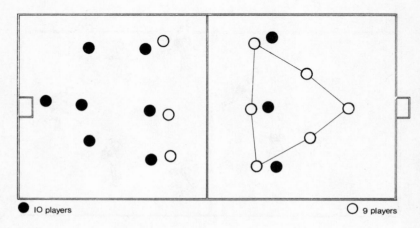

● IO players   ○ 9 players

4   Games for Testing Skill

123   **Hit the Box**

No. of players: Twelve.
Purpose :   To improve accuracy of hitting.
Structure of   Players place themselves opposite their partners
practice: around a circle in the centre of which is a 'box' 1 yd
                     square. Players have to hit the ball through the box
                     to their partners.
Coaching points: Basic hitting technique.
                     Receiving the ball.
Winner: The pair who get the most shots through the box in
                     a given time.

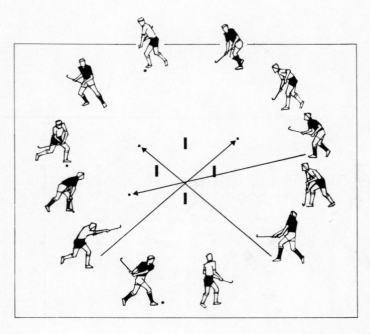

Shuttle Race

No. of players:	Four to ten.
Purpose:	To improve control when fatigued.
Structure of practice:	From the halfway line to the 25 yd line flags or markers are placed at 5 yd intervals. Players line up on the halfway line with a ball each. They move two flags forwards and one back, moving first backwards with the ball in front of them, then two forwards and one back until they reach the 25 yd line on their fourth forward run. They then repeat the exercise until they reach the halfway line.
Coaching points:	Footwork to get quick change of direction. Ball out in front of body to allow fast forward running.
Winner:	The first player back to the halfway line.

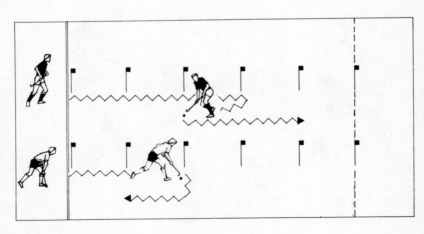

125   Slalom

No. of players: Two.

Purpose: To improve ball control when fatigued.

Structure of practice: A slalom course is set out over a 25 yd area. The player goes through the slalom round the end post and back through the slalom to the start point. He rests for the time it took him to go through the slalom and then repeats the exercise, resting after the second run. He then does a third slalom which is record run. He then does a third slalom which is timed. The total of the Run — Rest — Run — Rest — Run — Rest are taken. Second player, who has been timing, then does the exercise.

Coaching points: Body position for close control. Speed when turning.

Winner: The player with the shortest time for the whole sequence.

Shooting Competition

No. of players:	Four to six.
Purpose:	To improve shooting ability.
Structure of practice:	A player stands inside the circle with six balls placed behind a line 3 yd outside the circle. On the command 'Go' the player moves back to collect the first ball, dribbles it into the circle and shoots at the goal with a push or hit (method to be selected by the coach). The goal is marked with two posts placed 18 inches inside the posts. Points are scored as shown in the diagram below. Other players stand ready to collect the balls and return them. Players move round taking a turn each.
Coaching points:	Technique of hitting or pushing on the run to shoot at goal.
Winner:	The player who scores most points in the minimum time.

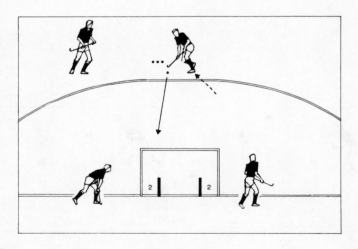

No. of players:	Five or six.
Purpose:	To improve pushing accuracy at speed.
Structure of practice:	A player stands in front of a line behind which six balls are placed 3 yd away. Three gates 1 yd wide are placed 10 yd from the line. On the command 'Go' the player moves to get the first ball and plays it at the first gate. After playing the first ball at the gate he moves for the second and so on until all six balls have been played. Two balls are played at each gate.
Coaching points:	Footwork to move quickly to collect ball. Moving ball and getting into correct pushing position for accuracy and power.
Winner:	As for game 126. One point is scored each time a ball passes through a gate.

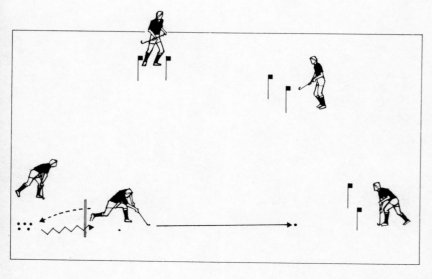

128 Hitting Through Gate

No. of players:	Five.
Purpose:	To improve accuracy of hitting.
Structure of practice:	A player stands in an area 4 x 4 yd at the junction of the halfway line and side-line. Six balls are placed 1 yd outside the box as in the illustration below. Three gates each 2 yd wide are placed approximately 20 yd from the player. Behind each goal a fielder is placed to collect the balls. The player performing the exercise must remain in the box for the duration of the exercise. He reaches with his stick in his left hand

to get the first ball, draws it across into the hitting position and hits it through one of the gates. The exercise is repeated with the six balls, two being played to each gate. One point is scored each time a ball goes through a gate.

Coaching points: Left-hand position of stick to pull ball in from outside the box. Change of hand position for hit. Footwork to get into hitting position. Follow through to give power and accuracy.

Winner: As for game 127.

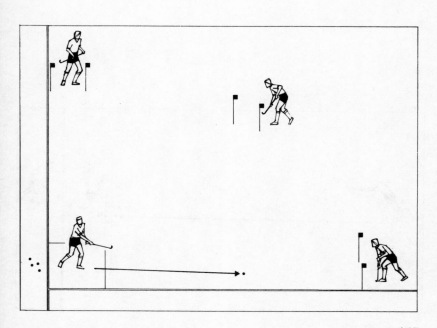

129   Control in the Box

No. of players:	Three.
Purpose:	To improve control when receiving the ball.
Structure of practice:	A player stands inside an area approximately 1 x 3 yd. A player serving the ball stands 20 yd away while a third player stands behind the control box to field any ball not controlled. The server hits the ball at the player in the box who must control it within the area of the box. One point is scored each time the ball is stopped within the box.
Coaching points:	Hand positions on stick for effective control. Footwork to get body into good position for controlling the ball. Stick to be in position to avoid rebound of ball.
Winner:	The player who controls the greatest number of shots within the area.

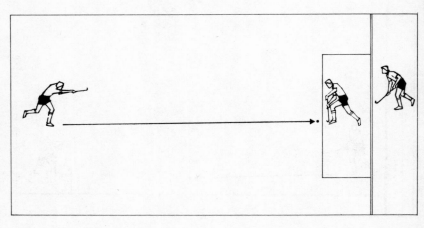

Aerial Contest

No. of players:	Two.
Purpose:	To improve the ability to give an aerial pass.
Structure of practice:	Two players stand from 15 to 20 yd away from each other, one starting with the ball. The player with the ball attempts to flick the ball over the head of his partner. The partner waits for the ball to land and then attempts to flick it from where it lands, back over the head of his partner. The players continue in this way until one of the players gets the ball over the side-line behind his partner.
Coaching points:	Particular attention should be given to lower the centre of gravity: a strong right hand and forearm movement and keeping the ball in contact with the stick as long as possible.
Winner:	The player who forces his opponent back to the side line the greatest number of times.

131   Shooting

No. of players:	Seven.
Purpose:	To improve shooting.
Structure of practice:	Two flags are placed 5 yd outside the circle opposite the 10 yd mark on the goal-line. If required to indicate where players must shoot from, two areas can be marked just inside the circle, as shown in the diagram. Player A, who is shooting, stands on the far side of the marker flag from the goal. The server feeds the ball between the flag and the circle for A to run on to collect and move into the circle to shoot. As the goalkeeper clears the ball, or a goal is scored, the second server flicks the ball to player B. Two players stand behind the goal to field the balls. Change players round after six shots for each player.
Coaching points:	Receive the ball without a break in forward movement. Shoot as soon as entering the circle. Shoot off either foot.
Winner:	The player who scores most goals in six attempts.

132   Reverse Stick Pass

No. of players:	Two to six.
Purpose:	To improve accuracy in reverse stick passing.
Structure of practice:	A marker is placed in the centre of a 10 yd square. At either end three balls are placed in the centre of the line. On each side-line a gate 1 yd wide is placed, both gates being slightly off centre, as in the diagram below. A player dribbles the first ball to the left of the centre marker. As he passes the marker he makes a reverse stick pass through gate A. He continues on to the far line to collect another ball, again moving to his left of the marker; as he passes the marker he reverse stick passes the ball through gate B. He continues the sequence until all the balls have been played and he has returned to the start line.
Coaching points:	Technique for running at speed with the ball. Change of stick position to pass effectively from reverse side. Position of ball in relation to body when passed to get maximum power.
Winner:	As for game 127.

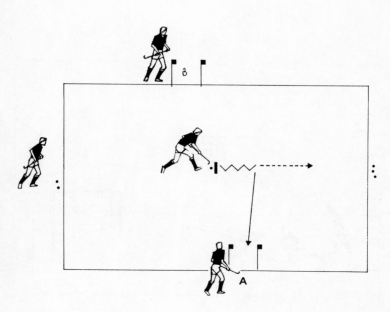

133   Penalty Stroke

No. of players:	Two to six.
Purpose:	To improve accuracy in taking penalty strokes.
Structure of practice:	A goal is marked as a wall (or string can be used to divide an ordinary goal in sections as shown below). Six attempts are made by a player to flick the ball through the marked areas from a spot 7 yd out from the centre of the goal. Points are scored as shown by the numbers in the squares below. The ball must not touch the ground between being flicked and crossing the goal-line.
Coaching points:	Low flicking position to get power, with good follow through for accuracy. Ensure a well-timed transfer of weight from the right leg to the left in the movement.
Winner:	The player who scores the greatest number of points in six attempts.

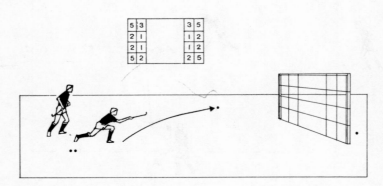

No. of Players: Two to six.
Purpose: To improve the accuracy of hitting or pushing out for
                      a penalty corner, and handstopping.
Structure of   A player pushes six balls along the ground, or hits
practice: them, from the 10 yd mark to the right or left of the
                      goal through a gate 2 ft wide which is 4 yd in from
                      the crown of the circle. A second player stands on the
                      edge of the circle and moves in to hand stop each
                      ball. A pair working from the left can alternate with a
                      pair working from the right. The ball must be played
                      firmly and pass through the gate for the attempt to
                      count. Each player scores a point for playing the ball
                      through the gate and for handstopping correctly.
                      Each player has six attempts from each side at hand-
                      stopping and hitting (or pushing).
Coaching points: Specific hitting or pushing positions to get ball out
                      firmly and accurately. Hand stopper controlling ball
                      with left hand outside the line of the left foot.
Winner: The player who scores most points.

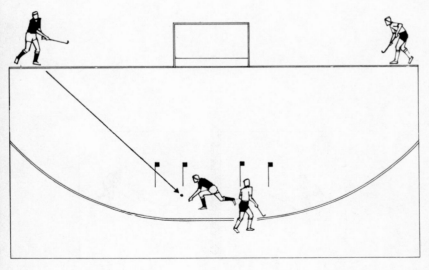

5   Miscellaneous Games

135   Hockey Tennis: Singles

No. of players: Two.
Purpose: To improve giving a first time pass.
Structure of   Two players play either side of a net in an area
practice: 5 x 10 yd with a net about 2 ft 6 in high. The ball has
                   to land within the playing area and may only bounce
                   once. Players score each time they win a point. To
                   start the game the ball must be flicked or scooped
                   from the back line.
Coaching points: Emphasize footwork to move quickly. Hand position
                   on stick to get a controlled shot into opponent's end
                   of court.
Winner: First player to score nine points wins the game. Three
                   games form a set.

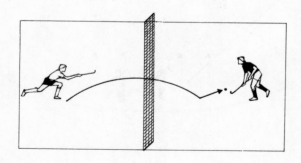

136 **Hockey Tennis: Doubles**

No. of players: Four.
Purpose: To improve giving a first time pass.
Structure of   Two teams of two in an area 10 yd square with a net
practice: about 2 ft 6 in high across the centre. Rules as for
                   game 135.
Coaching points: As for game 135.
Winner: First team to score fifteen points wins the game.
                   Three games constitute a set.

No. of players:	Six or eight.
Purpose:	To improve a first time pass.
Structure of practice:	Two teams of three or four play in an area 10 x 10 yd over a net about 2 ft 6 in high across the centre. Playing rules as in game 135.
Coaching points:	As in game 135.
Winner:	First team to score 21 points wins the game. Three games constitute a set.

Hockey Cricket

No. of players: Nine to twelve.
Purpose: To improve skills generally.
Structure of   A pitch 20 yd long has wickets placed at either end.
practice: Two players bat at any time as in cricket. They must
                   run if they hit the ball. The ball is flicked to the
                   batsman by a player at the opposite end of the pitch.
                   The fielders hit the ball back and a batsman can be
                   run out by any fielder playing the ball against the
                   stumps with his stick. A player is out if a fielder
                   catches the ball on his stick from a full pitch or on
                   the first bounce. Players take it in turns to deliver
                   six balls from each end. Players bat in turn.
Coaching points: Various skill elements according to role of the player
                   within the game.
Winner: The player who finishes with the greatest number of
                   runs.

No. of players:	Two.
Purpose:	To improve first time pass and control.
Structure of practice:	Two players play the ball against a wall over a low line (say 2 ft 6 in). The ball is allowed to bounce once only before being played. A ball played below the line or allowed to bounce more than once loses a point.
Coaching points:	Hand positions for controlling the ball against the wall. Footwork to get into position before shot is played. Deception to try to get opponent wrong-footed.
Winner:	The first player to score eleven points. Three games constitute a set.